FINDING SPIRIT IN PRISON INMATES DREAMS

Carol Oschmann

Author's Tranquility Press
MARIETTA, GEORGIA

Copyright © 2021 by Carol Oschmann

All rights reserved. No part of this publication may be reproduced, distributed or transmitted in any form or by any means, including photocopying, recording, or other electronic or mechanical methods, without the prior written permission of the publisher, except in the case of brief quotations embodied in critical reviews and certain other noncommercial uses permitted by copyright law. For permission requests, write to the publisher, addressed "Attention: Permissions Coordinator," at the address below.

Carol Oschmann/Author's Tranquility Press
2706 Station Club Drive SW
Marietta, GA 30060
www.authorstranquilitypress.com

Ordering Information:
Quantity sales. Special discounts are available on quantity purchases by corporations, associations, and others. For details, contact the "Special Sales Department" at the address above.

Finding Spirit in Prison Inmates Dreams/ Carol Oshmann
Paperback   ISBN: 978-1-957208-28-2
EBook   ISBN: 978-1-957208-29-9

Disclaimer

All names, places and some situations have been changed to protect the dreamer's identity.

Other books by Carol Oschmann

When God Stood Up – a memoir detailing what happened when God come alive in her life; a physical healing, the steps that led to her spiritual gift of dreaming for others. There's a lot she learned about life after death in her encounters with various people and the heartaches Spirit solved.

Biblical Dream Study – nonfiction, takes the 134 times dreams are mentioned in the Bible and discusses with you the lessons that are meant for us.

Overboard on Lake Ontario – fiction, middle grade with teachers' guidelines if wanted. Tom, a homeless boy sets out to show his value to the marina owner. Drug runners, bullies, boat fires, murders shake the world he wants to be a part of. How does he overcome them?

Small business advertisers, Brochures subjects; beginning a spirit filled path; life after death, alternatives to suicide, hope, prison dreams – free for samples, 100 for donation to waiting rooms, nursing homes, funeral homes, good way to advertise your business and help others. $25.00

To share, ask for an interpretation, or purchase author signed paper-backs; caroloschmann.com
or email a request to; oschmann@verizon.net

Subject line; Dreams

Prison Dreams Endorsements

While on a mission at the federal prison in Balm, Florida, I asked one of the female inmates if she had met Carol Oschmann, the author of this book. She told me that she had taken her class and had shared that she had not had dreams for many years. Carol asked her to go to a childhood dream. Carol then helped her figure out a life-long mystery.
Sister Roseanne Fogarty OSM

I found Carol's class on dreams extremely interesting even though I was already a member of her group. I've learned a lot that I can use. Wish this sort of class had been available years ago it would have saved me years of discomfort!
Arnold C. Larson (Jake), retired Mental Health Tech. Columbia, S. C.

Carol brought to my attention the difference between my ego consciousness and my subconscious. My ego is where I'm conditioned by what others say trying to fit in. Sure some is the true me but a lot is my conditioning to fit in. I'm learning to be the true Billie through Carol's work and finding messages from my subconscious. This is the aha. I feel the whole world can use this if they are open to it. She is a wonderful speaker/ instructor/ friend.
Billie Laurin, former Inmate.

Contents

Part One : Prison Stories

Chapter One 14

Chapter Two 22

Chapter Three 28

Chapter Four 33

Chapter Five 39

Chapter Six 47

Chapter Seven 56

Chapter Eight 64

Chapter Nine 71

Chapter Ten 77

Chapter Eleven 84

Chapter Twelve 89

Chapter Thirteen 99

Chapter Fourteen 104

Chapter Fifteen 108

Chapter Sixteen 113

Chapter Seventeen 117

Chapter Eighteen 120

Chapter Nineteen 124

Chapter Twenty 126

Chapter Twenty-One 130

Chapter Twenty-Two 134

Chapter Twenty-Three 138

Chapter Twenty-Four 141

Chapter Twenty-Five 146

Chapter Twenty-Six 149

Chapter Twenty-Seven 154

Chapter Twenty-Eight 158

Chapter Twenty-Nine 161

Part Two: Dream Work

Chapter Thirty 166

Chapter Thirty-One 174

Chapter Thirty-Two 179

Chapter Thirty-Three 184

Chapter Thirty-Four 189

Chapter Thirty-Five 195

Chapter Thirty-Six 200

INTRODUCTION

You are in for an amazing, cutting-edge experience. The number of people doing dream in work in prison in a group, around the globe, can be counted on one hand. However, the number of people doing serious dream work on themselves grows daily.

This book is taken from the time I've spent volunteering in a women's prison doing dream work in a group setting. You don't have to be a dream worker to appreciate the life changing power of the stories contained in this book.

What do we really know about life? How much do we know about our inner life? Why do we sometimes do what we do, some-times feel as we feel? What do we know about the inner lives of those who've made mistakes, such as the people in prison? Is it possible to change their thinking, make things better for them when they get out? Can using this tool of dreams possibly lead to true rehabilitation in prison, or change your own life for the better?

If you've grown up unhappy, wanting more out of life yet clueless how to get it and maybe doubtful you deserve better; this book will endeavor to change your mind. It you believe the words of the adult figures in your life who've said you were worthless; this book will endeavor to change your mind. If you believe your only path is to zone out on drugs; this book will endeavor to change your mind.

Psychologist Carl G. Jung taught, "We are like icebergs floating on the ocean of life." The only part of ourselves we are aware of is the small part that floats above the waterline, our ego. This is the part that interacts with parents, teachers, siblings, neighbors, TV. It molds who we'll become, how we'll think, and tries to guide our path.

Floating under the water, our unconscious self, also tries to guide our path. It's the area where all the happenings in our life, which we don't want to think about, are buried. It's the part where memories of everything we've experience, seen, or read are stored. It also contains our connection with our true self; our higher self who knows who we came into this world to be. Artist Salvador Dali has done a painting of this with the part of 'I' being an 'eye.'

Do we listen to the people on the surface of life's ocean, or do we get in tune with our hidden, inner self? If you don't come to know your hidden, inner self, it can cause you much trouble. When you become familiar with the unconscious self, you'll experience joy. Life is full of choices. Our creator gave us the power of free will. To me, choosing to listen, interpret, find meaning in your nightly messages is the biggest choice we have.

Please get to know the inner you. It's not taking another look at all those things you've tried to forget. It's going deeper to the real you and letting that inner voice come through. Sometimes dreams use those things you want to forget, sending you warnings of events or people about to come into your life and allowing you to avoid heartache.

There is much to learn from understanding yourself. You can find the inner help you need to make important decisions in life and bring about the miracles you deserve. This book particularly addresses reforming prison inmates, however, there are prisons we create ourselves, with mental bars. There is also a section on leading a group such as I've described in this book. You might want to use this information to start a group in your neighborhood before you venture into a prison. You picked up the book! Everything happens for a reason. Hopefully, this will be your path to happiness and fulfillment.

Carol Oschmann

PART ONE

Prison Stories

CHAPTER ONE

Not ten miles from my home is a faith- and character-based women's prison. I thought that I'd like to try doing dream work there. My inspiration came from two friends, Rev. Jeremy Taylor and Pat Gavin who have both worked in similar institutions.

Jeremy has three dream schools of his own. One is in California, one in Mexico, and one in Korea. He also teaches about dreams at the Haden Institute in Hendersonville, North Carolina. He is a minister and the author of several dream related books. He taught dream work in San Quentin with much success and encourages everyone he teaches to get involved.

Pat is a very small, delicate appearing lady, who is leading a group in Attica Prison in upstate New York. Her full-time job is with the Veterans Administration. This led her to want to help veterans in prison who are also doing life sentences for serious crimes. She won the president Jefferson Award in 2008 for her work. One man's family was so grateful for her part in reuniting a father with his children that they recommended her for the award. She gives credit to the dream work.

I took on women prisoners rather than men because I felt more comfortable with women. Many people are in prisons, the concrete ones in our justice system or in one of our own makings. These people can benefit greatly, quickly from personal dream study. Dreams accelerate during times of stress and/or change. Dreams bring messages from your inner self to better your life whether you need help in making decisions, improving your health, anything. Nothing is too big or too small. If you're not happy, neither is your soul – and it wants to be happy! It knows how. Studying dreams is well worth the time!

One can find peace and happiness, even in jail. Accept and cope. Dealing with your dreams lets you know you are never truly alone. The dreams come from someone within yourself, your higher self, God, Spirit, whatever name you wish to use. You can trust this someone completely because this someone knows all about you, loves you and wants the best for you no matter what's in your past.

After deciding I wanted to help bring peace and happiness to women prisoners the big question was how do I get the prison chaplain to let me in? One Tampa Tribune article featured a story about a lady who taught art at our nearby prison. The last line indicated that the chaplain was looking for volunteers. The article stated that if you had a specialty you wished to share you could give her a call. I did.

Before calling I made a few notes about my qualification, my degree, my book, my ongoing dream group, and my two friends who do dream work in prisons. Then I picked up the phone and explained all this to the prison chaplain. Unknown to me was the fact that the women sleep in compounds and when one has a nightmare, they all lose sleep. The whole compound population might be sleep deprived the next day making them angry and sick. I'd called at just the right time offering hope, because there was a woman who was having nightmares. Then again, in my point of view, all timing is God's timing.

The chaplain did a background check on me, returned my call and the next week we were meeting face to face. She joked we'd probably have 1500 women, prisoners, guards and volunteers wanting to take the class. (There are three hundred beds in this prison.) The regular class cycle is twelve weeks. Presumably the present class would graduate, and I'd get a new class at the end of twelve weeks. Since I had said I prefer 15 people at a time, she decided on three from each compound for the first class. After graduating, they'd be able to form dream groups in their compounds. The dream work could spread that way, and I'd have a fresh class of prisoners every twelve weeks. That was the way we hoped it would work. The next week I was teaching my first class.

Walking into the prison the first time was not too bad. I was expected and a guard walked me to the chaplain's office. The orientation, however, was scary.

In the preprinted manual I read never to bring gifts to the inmates. Each time I came to the prison I would be given a pocket alarm to use if, and when, I felt threatened. The chaplain told me what to do if I was taken hostage or witnessed a disturbing incident.

Well, I wanted to volunteer in a prison, so what did I expect?

The first class made all the little inconveniences seem worth it. The eager, hopeful faces of the women and the dream images they related were ones I'd never get on the outside. It appears the dreams themselves knew I was coming and had popped up just to help me understand each girl in her present state. But, of course, this is true. Everything happens in the dream before it happens in life, better known as de-ja vu.

These women held a lot of hidden potential – good tendencies that had not had a chance to see the light of day. Dreams are stronger when we are stressed.

I couldn't (because of prisoner confidentiality) know what they had done. I often watch the news and wonder if I could be unbiased about certain crimes; however, for this work, I find it more helpful for them if I can let the dreams offer hope, a different view of themselves than they'd been holding. I don't interpret the dreams. The group works the dream until the dreamer has what we call an "ah-ha" feeling.

When we strike gold, a truth about the dreamer's self hits her in the face, then we move on to the next dream. Dreams do hold more than one message, but I feel that one revelation at a time is enough for most people to handle. It takes a lot of thought to digest that one piece of information. The important thing is realizing the revelations come from inside themselves. Then a difference in their life is made.

One young woman's dream tells a lot. "I had to go to the morgue to identify my boyfriend's dead body. I walk in, a drawer is pulled out. A sheet covered body lies there. I lift the sheet. 'Yes,' I say. I have no emotion. "That's him.' His mother is in the corner acting like a crazy woman, screaming and crying. You know ...like a mother would do under the circumstances. I turn to leave, and I'm drawn to another drawer in the wall. I pull this one out myself and inside it is a live, happy, playing baby. I close the drawer and leave. Outside the room I change my mind, turn and go back inside. Now my dead boyfriend is alive and playing with the baby!"

My first question was, "Is your boyfriend dead?"

"No," she replied. "And please don't tell me I'm going to get back with the x#*x@x! And no baby! Uh-uh! No baby, not with that bad dude!"

"This could be a prediction." I noted glumly. "But let's try to find some symbolic meaning. Dreams use what you know to tell you what you don't know."

This is a favorite saying of Rev. Jeremy Taylor. I wrote the key words of the dream on the blackboard, and we started doing word association. Boyfriend, morgue, mother, crazy, uncover, baby, drawer, and my hands were the words I wrote on the board.

"Can you give me three words to describe your boyfriend?" I asked.

"Crazy, loving (I know that sounds like opposites but true) and undependable." This was her answer.

I felt I was in trouble. "I should have explained a little better," I said. "All people and all things in the dream are or can be a part of you. What you described is yourself." And, not knowing her, I held my breath.

"You got that right!" she shouted out. They all laughed as I made a wiping the sweat off the brow motion.

"Thank you for being so honest," I added.

"If he is you, that part of you that he represents is dead. That can be good or bad. You're shown a male instead of a female so I'd guess that making a living, developing a talent, being responsible for your decisions is part of what he represents in you. Now look to your life and see what is there that you need to wake up to.

"You described the mother as crazy also. She is you, the side of you that should be nurturing, helping someone or something to grow. Instead, she confirms a craziness in how you're neglecting something that may be good for you. If it's something bad in yourself that needs airing, you may need to bring it into the open and deal with it." I was making guesses, hoping I'd hit a memory in her.

The great part of working dreams in a group is that only the dreamer knows the truth when it hits. She gets that "ah-ha" feeling deep inside. If often takes many guesses from many different people until this happens.

Having been invited from the beginning to make comments at any time, one of the other women shouted out, "And she's got herself backed into a corner!" They knew each other and this brought out a lot of "That's right!" and more laughter. She agreed.

"What does the baby signify?" asked another.

"If it were my dream," I began, "a baby usually signifies a new life, a new opportunity to take something out of the drawer of life and work on it. This is not a brand-new baby. It's sitting up and playing. It's probably a talent that you are aware of. It probably is something you know you can easily do but have not pursued developing it yet."

"You're singing!" More than a few voices rang out.

The dreamer was looking extremely pleased. I find there are often talents hidden within us that were belittled in our childhood. We were told these talents were not a practical way to make a living. We totally ignored them feeling everyone else has the same talent or better. Yet, if this talent was meant to be a major part of her life it would bubble in her subconscious, creating trouble for her in the outer world until she nurtured this talent, practiced it, perfected it.

She said she was scheduled to be released soon and if she didn't come back to class, be assured she would be eternally grateful for this insight. She could see that her inner self (higher self) was giving her permission to be who she really wanted to be.

"It's in your hands," I told her. "You can open or close the drawers yourself. Right now, it's in a place of death. To fulfill your destiny, get it out into the open, work with it, improve it. Those were your hands on the drawers. You'll find your life taking a better, dramatic turn."

All of the seven or eight dreams we discussed that night brought looks of amazement to the women's faces. It turned into a blur for me. I vowed to find a way to remember better so others could benefit from hearing these stories. There are more dreams and more detail in later prison visits. I was so overwhelmed with emotion myself that it was the next morning before I could share some of it with my husband.

In each class it's necessary to spend some of the time teaching. This first night I told a little of my story, my physical healing, the many attitude changes I went through, but I centered on nightmares. I call my 'midlife crises' a difficult period that led me to dream study.

I explained how illness gives you time to get your life on a better path. Although most of them are much younger than I, without the illness, I explained how the problem that landed them in jail is also giving them the time to learn about themselves, and the time to change and become who they came into this world to be. If they learn about themselves sufficiently, they may someday even be glad for this experience, and they wouldn't have to have a mid-life crisis. They'd get on the right path sooner and could do better for the world than I'll have time to do.

As they were filing out, one young lady asked if I could talk more about handling nightmares next time. She said that as a child, she'd been shot in the head and suffered nightmares from it ever since. It was then I noticed her prosthetic eye.

Relating this to my grandchildren a few weeks later, we all agreed that we have no problems! The chaplain called later in the week to tell me that several lives were changed that night.

CHAPTER TWO

The second night at prison, no one handed me the safety button to take to class. I'd been told by the chaplain that the guards would provide me with this devise for my own protection. In my eagerness to get to class, I also forgot to ask for it. That night my teaching centered on nightmares as I had promised. I told them to wake themselves up and face the monsters in their head and ask, "What do you want of me?" Then go back to sleep holding that image in their minds.

I related how one group of demons used to attack me on a regular basis. If my husband was there, they fled. When I would go to bed alone, they came. I was at my wit's end. I'd been doing a lot of dream study and trying to follow my dreams. Many good things had happened in my life. This one night I yelled out at God (it may have just been an internal scream) I said, "Take these things away! Tell me what I need to know some other way!"

God took them away. They never returned.

I talked about how snakes used to be my demons. Snakes went from being enemies, to punishing me for my sins, to becoming my friends by warning me before-hand of potential problems.

I talked of a possible correlation between daytime happenings and night-time dreams. At one point in my study I'd used a calendar to color code my nights and days. This way I could look for patterns of things that I was thinking, doing, or saying wrong from habit. It also helped track the predictions and the warnings.

This calendar had helped me so much. I printed some and handed them out to my class. On the calendar I also included some astrological moon signs. The moon changes every three days. It governs the tides, our feminine monthly cycles and possibly our mood swings and even dreams. As an example, I found a correlation with the sign of Pisces that I didn't like. Every month, when the moon entered the Pisces position I had a bad day.

Did you ever have a day when you got up in a bad mood and it went downhill from there? This is the kind of day I mean. I'd drop things, stumble, hurt myself, couldn't seem to do anything right. I began to dread this time of month as much as that other time of month, before menopause. My husband and I decided to pack a picnic the next time Pisces was arriving and take a long ride in the car. Nothing could ruin a day like that, we reasoned. We were right. We had a great day and Pisces never bothered me again.

I was able to break the pattern it brought me by simply being aware it might happen and doing something, like a long ride and a picnic. These things I truly enjoy. Actually, there were other bad patterns I needed to face and this was a good lesson for me.

I gave them all the tools I had. It would be interesting to see if any of them found a pattern in their life from the moon's forces also.

Then we did as many dreams as possible. One that stood out in my memory was from a girl (I'm guessing her age at 25 or 26) who told of having a dream at age 13, that she was being raped by the devil. I saw that dream as a prediction, an event that might have been changed, had the people around her believed in dreams and discussed them over breakfast.

As it was, at age fourteen she was raped and subsequently gave birth to her first baby. She had two more children under similar circumstances, the last being born in prison. Why she's there, I have no clue. The fact remains, each of her three children are being raised by different families and may never get to know each other. I can imagine the added pain and trauma that she goes through each day in prison as someone else talks about their visits with their children and passes around pictures of them. Her anger showed as she told her latest dream.

"I'm called to the visitor's area to visit with my three children," she said. "In reality, they would never visit me and if they did, they would never come together. In my dream, the two oldest were younger than they really are, perhaps they look as I remember them last time I saw them. My youngest baby, in the dream, is fourteen. Two of my prison friends are told to go with me to the visitor's area. When the children leave, one of my friends begins cussing me out. I'm surprised because this friend doesn't cuss."

"Do you swear at yourself?" I asked, thinking the friend was really a part of her. Several of the women said she does that all the time. Together we speculated this dream was about an eventual coming together. The girls pointed out the coincidence of the youngest being fourteen, one coming together and four family members becoming another fourteen. Fourteen years until they all get together?

She said that was how much time was left on her sentence.

The dream is one of many I took home and had some further insights during the week.

The next morning, I woke with the added information that the dream was like the old carrot and stick story. This seems to be an obsession of hers, to be all together. Possibly a reunion was being held out as a promise if she recognized something else of importance in her life. We'd have to follow her next dreams to get a clue as to what she needed to change. I felt she should look at those two friends, see what she likes and doesn't like about them and work on those things in herself. The woman had been so depressed that I was eager to give her something positive to hang onto. I called the chaplain and asked her to forward this information to the dreamer as it would give her that positive something to work on. She said she would.

During that same class, another dreamer tells of going into a strange compound to visit a girlfriend. "After getting in the door, I stop short. There are only men in here. They are nice enough, so I ask which bed does my friend sleep in? They point to the bed." That was all she could remember.

Not much to go on. Looking for a bed seemed odd so I asked her to close her eyes and become the bed. I asked her to answer the questions as if she was the bed.

"Describe yourself as that bed." I directed.

"I'm brass, with spindles" she replied.

The prison beds are much simpler than that.

"What do you like about being that bed?" I asked.

"I have a purpose. I make life easier for me."

"What do you not like about being that bed," I asked next.

"I'm too close to the bathroom." She replied.

Ah-ha, I thought. A clue.

"What would you be if you could be any bed you wanted to be?" I asked.

"I'd be in a big bedroom with lots of pretty comforters on me." She said.

I told her, "If it were my dream, being near the bathroom gives me an opportunity to get rid of some wrong attitude I have. To me bathrooms are about eliminating something."

"How do I know which attitude is wrong?" she asked.

"Just keep an open mind. Admit you don't know everything. It happens without you doing anything. You don't get to pick and choose between your many attitudes. You often don't realize you've changed your heart on something," I said. "You know something's changed when, in the dream, you're going to the bathroom in a public place. It's a real biggy if you're naked." They laughed. "You're not hiding anything anymore.

One interesting thing is that one day you'll be thinking: Boy! A few months ago, that would have bothered me!" I added.

Often, the biggest lesson will come in the briefest dream image.

All the dreams were memorable that night and in two hours we were able to cover most of them.

Other messages also became clearer to me as the week progressed.

Later that week, the local newspaper ran a photo and an article about a group creating stained glass windows and such. Here was a clue to the meaning of the bed dream. Wow! Stained glass people use brass as a bonding agent! The glue that holds life together for that last dreamer is in the foundation of the bed, the vehicle we use most to receive dreams. To me, that's dream work. I didn't call the chaplain. That revelation would be fun sharing at the next class. I took it as a dream lesson for me as much as for her. My work was being approved by a higher authority!

CHAPTER THREE

The third class almost ended my career as a volunteer prison dream coach. In my zeal to give all I knew to fight the demons in dreams to the lady who'd been shot as a child, I'd included a calendar with astrological signs. Before going to my third class, I called the chaplain to see if I needed to let her know that I was bringing in more handouts.

"You can bring handouts but let me ask you one thing," she said. "Don't use the handout with the astrological signs. It gets them spending energy on something not necessary."

"Okay," I replied. I should have known. The devil made me do it? The chaplain had said in our initial interview that most of the inmates were new to Christianity, and she didn't want me to confuse them by introducing anything but Carl Jung psychology. I suppose she equated him with science.

That night, several of the girls came in with Bibles in their hands that they kept thumbing through. We had a trustee taking the class who others told me from the start abused her small amount of power. They wished she was not in the class, and I was soon to find out why.

When I announced we'd do away with the calendar, a small controversy ensued. Some women wanted it. Despite the strain we did some dreams but before our two hours were up, the trustee admitted to raising the objection to the astrological signs, calling it witchcraft, and got into a shouting match with the other girls. The girls who wanted the calendar said they were tired of being preached to and being told what to believe. They countered that the wise men were astrologers! God made the stars. Astrology is a science. The moon governed their menstrual flows so why not learn more about it when they had a chance? It got loud.

There I was without an alarm button to push. I wasn't scared as they seemed to be sensitive to my wishes to stop the argument. Each side had many things they needed to say, things to get out in the open. One woman stayed by the door admitting she was afraid. The trustee left and things quieted down.

The chaplain had asked for two copies of my book, <u>God Speaks In Dreams; Connect With Him And Each Other</u>, for the prison library, which the trustee took with her. Now my goose is really cooked, I thought. The chaplain will read my various controversial views and stop the class. All week I waited for the phone to ring with the chaplain at the other end saying I couldn't come back. The call didn't come. Then, again, I thought, it probably takes more than a week to read the book.

So, let's get back to the good that happened that night.

Our lady with the three children in three different homes, who dreamed about meeting all of them in the visitor's area had a new dream to report. The dream upset her yet she laughed at it because it seemed to have no basis in reality at all. She wished it did. "In the dream," she said, "I just got out of prison and I went to claim the house my grandmother left to me in a will." (This is the part that never happened. No grandmother, no will, no house.) She went on. "When I get there, I found out someone has taken possession of the house and is auctioning it off. I'm devastated! I go up a winding staircase so I can be seen and heard and proceed to yell and fight for my property."

This brought a lot of comments from the ladies and the dreamer herself. The little battle about the calendars earlier that night hadn't helped me be able to hold the floor. That night, I often seemed to lose control. Finally, I got through to her that this story was the same as last week. She is fighting for something she wants very badly. Last week it was the children she was fighting for and this week the house.

"I want to get out!" she said. "I want a home!" We agreed that was probably part of it. The dream seems to be telling her how to accomplish these goals – or not.

Not all dreams can be solved right away and this seemed an installment in a dream series with more information to come. We didn't have a complete story to work with. God often tells us little bits at a time trying to persuade us to take steps in a different direction, hoping to make something clearer. We must cross certain intersections on our path before the dreams can mold our attitudes. As was once said, take one step at a time.

If the dreamer recognizes one image in the dream they can work on, that is enough for now. Some prisoners' tiny steps forward are small wars won. What was witnessed in this class seemed enormous to all of us in the room! Actually, one dream can bring more than one message. What you miss will repeat in another dream at a later time.

Another prisoner told a dream of meeting her boyfriend and being given a gift of a candle holder shaped like a clown. The clown held out his hands for the votive. "My boyfriend gave me the gift and then we embraced." The other women made sure I knew this boyfriend was not to be confused with her husband.

"If it was my dream and I was the clown," I say, "I'm holding a light in my hands. I'm lighting the way for others. A clown may be saying to put some fun in your life." Another inmate said she was afraid of clowns and reminded us of a movie where the clown was evil. I thought about having her become the clown but didn't do that. The mood the rest were in could prove brutal for her.

As I explained to my husband, later, perhaps the marriage was a mistake; maybe he's abusive, maybe a lot of things. Ever practical, Jim's reply was, "Why the heck would she want to be involved with another man?" He was probably closer to the truth of the dream.

During one session, though, I was trying to convince her she was more, her dreams were pointing to herself as more than what she thought. The men, the gifts were surface things. We had to look deeper. It was fairly chaotic, and I was not feeling in control.

I had hoped to find a way to remember more stories, sensing they would provide good examples to future classes. That wasn't going to happen tonight. I was shocked and wondering if I could even continue this seemingly helpful mission. The chaplain had told me twice now that lives had been changed as a result of the dream study, so I couldn't give up.

One more revelation was to be made to me as the girls filed out of the room that night. Many of them gave me hugs, sympathizing with me over this controversy my calendar had caused. Halfway through, the lady who'd been shot as a child and suffered demons ever since, the one who'd indirectly caused this fracas said she'd done what I suggested. Soon after the last class, in the middle of the night after waking herself up, she yelled out at God to take away the demons, she did not need them. She had to do it three times that night, but after the third time they disappeared and never came back. Her bunk mate, waiting behind her, affirmed this.

Couldn't help it, but I felt soooo good. I thanked God all the way home!

CHAPTER FOUR

The fourth night (you know I couldn't wait until I'd been there so long I'd lost count!) I asked the lady with the demons, who'd gotten shot as a child, if the demons were still gone. "Yes!" she said. She told the story again of what she did. She added that she'd not recorded a dream since. She'd been too busy sleeping! Couldn't say I blamed her. I told her regular nightmares might come which should not be confused with the old demons. Nightmares are the best teaching tool we have. When something upsets us, we are more likely to do something to change it. We're more likely to change our minds, more importantly our hearts, and take a different path. The other inmates cheered for her.

"Enjoy your sleep for now, but pretty soon start encouraging more dreams. They may not be nightmares at all. If you try to follow your dreams, they will be interesting stories," I told her.

She did relate another dream, however, that had also come before removing her demons. "I'm marching in a straight line, in my prison clothes, inside barbed wire, under a canopy roof, next to a still body of water. It could be a pool (although we don't have a pool in prison), more likely it was a retention pond. The pond has dividers like competition swimming pools usually do, you know, those ropes and buoy balls. An ugly creature, snake-like, is swooshing around in the pond making the water murky. On the roof of the canopy is a pumpkin-headed man with my baby in his arms. My Uncle Frank is also there. The pumpkin-headed man jumps off the roof and into the pool with my baby. I'm terrified for my baby." That was the end of the dream. She added, "I know I didn't get the whole story."

We asked about her uncle and she said she thought of him as a protector. We all thought the canopy or roof was a protector also. We worked on the baby with the six magic questions. Her description, coming from the perspective of being the baby, was to be happy and make mom and dad proud. (Wow! Wonder what she thought of her parents and how they felt about where she was?) The next question was, what did she like about being that baby? She said she liked having the opportunity to learn more than she did the first time around. "I can do things differently!" she answered.

I asked, "What do you dislike about being that baby?"

She answered, "I dislike my feeling of helplessness."

I then asked, "What do you, the baby, fear the most or, what your biggest desire?"

She replied, "I don't think I can answer these questions because I'm too young to know about fear. I have no fear. And I don't really know that I have a right to make choices. I've got a lot to learn! Actually, I've gone through life just taking what life handed me."

She saw a lot of parallels in her life and the way she answered these questions. Make her parents proud! Do things over!

Since everything in the dream is a part of the dreamer, we talked about the pumpkin-headed man part of her. It was trying to take charge. Perhaps he symbolized her ego and how he was not ready to take charge because he had nothing but pulp between his ears. Again, she had things to learn about life, to replace that pulp. She, as the pumpkin-headed man, knew she wanted the baby – the chance to start over and she was getting it. A big desire can lead to a life lesson all by itself.

The creature in the water was also a part of her which was making things unclear, stirring up murk. She was causing her own unclear vision. Then again, as other people in the group pointed out, it was night and nothing was clear.

We try always to find some positive future or lesson and I was sure, having overcome her demons, she was well on her way to straightening out life so she could better attain what she wants. I look forward to her future dreams!

Another inmate related this dream:

"In my old neighborhood, where I lived when I was in the second grade, I met Charles T. He was a person I actually knew in second grade. He told me he was burning CDs with Becky H. and burned her house down. Becky is another person I knew in second grade! But, he bragged, he didn't get arrested!" End of dream.

She then told me she was in prison for arson. She said she lost everything in the fire, but she was accused and convicted of the crime. She said she didn't do it. Her sentence was two and a half years. I pointed out that this length of time corresponded with second grade.

She hasn't seen these people since second grade. She described Charles as being geekish, bald and someone others ridicule.

"Do these descriptions fit you?" I asked.

"All but the being bald," she answered. "Becky however, was the person I wanted to be. She was super nice, smart, and popular."

"You have those qualities in you. Becky in the dream is you." I pointed out that quite often a fire in a dream is cleansing. Out with the old, make room for the new. There is the myth of the Phoenix arising from the ashes. A grateful look came over her face at that. She liked the idea of a new beginning.

The image of a CD burning tickled me. I was once in a group of dream researchers commenting on how the world needed new myths and archetypes and what would they likely be. Rev. Jeremy Taylor found the children's toy, Transponders, as a modern myth because if it were in a child's dream it could signify all the different ways this person could be bent, snapped and turned into an entirely different being.

I saw the CD burning as a new myth or archetype. I asked what was the reason for burning a CD or DVD? The answer we all concurred on was the recording of new memories. How powerful is that when you sit in a prison! Time was soon coming for her to get this done. It wouldn't be long before she was back in the real world.

Another woman said that in her dream she was going to the Federal Court House to meet her boyfriend. She added a true life happening, he'd just been sent up on some kind of federal charges. Back in the dream, "on the courthouse steps a man stopped me, asked me if my name is _____ _____. I said, 'yes.' 'Here are your papers. You've been served!' he tells me. He added, 'You got five years in prison and four years' probation.' I'm confused because I already served five."

She didn't say what her crime was, but her total time was ten years. She has served five. I asked if there was any chance of getting out early, for good behavior or something. She just shrugged. First of all we told her to stay away from the courthouse. They all laughed. There wasn't much more we could do with this one, but decided in the next week we would reopen it and ask her to become the process server or maybe the steps.

The lady who'd lost her children and dreamed of losing her grandmother's house had another dream to report. "In this dream I'm being chased. As I run away, teeth fall out of my mouth with lots blood. My front teeth, top and bottom seem safe but the ones behind these keep falling into my hands. I didn't know I had so many teeth."

"Become one of the teeth. Describe yourself," I said.

She said, "I'm made of strong material."

"What is your purpose?" I asked.

She first said to chew her food and then added something very revealing. Her purpose was also to bite people, to provide defense.

"What do you like about being a tooth?" I asked.

She said, "Not much. I'm not doing my job. I feel defenseless. I'm falling and coated with blood."

It struck me as obvious. "You have no roots!" It was time for her to build roots and memories and the dreams would help pick the right ones. I also suggested that she could go back into the same dream and confront the person chasing her. She could ask him what he wanted and ask why she was losing her teeth.

I took this time to point out that all three dreams she's told us were about losing something valuable, her children, her grandmother's house and now her teeth.

"I think if it were my dream, that my unconscious self has fears of losing something greater than any of these," I said.

"What could be worse than losing your children?" she asked, tears in her eyes.

"How about losing your identity? Not as in identify theft but, really, losing your sense of who you are." I said.

She gasped and pointed to the woman next to her. "I was saying the same thing earlier today to her. It is so real!"

"Stick with your dreams," I said. "We'll find the real you yet." Sadly to say, she found the thought of changing her identity all too confusing and did not return.

CHAPTER FIVE

At the prison the next week, one young woman couldn't wait for everyone to gather to tell her story. Three weeks previously she's told a dream of an antique dresser with closed drawers. We'd suggested that she go back into that dream and open those drawers.

"Go to bed tonight," I had advised, "See that dresser again and see what's in the drawers. There could be a missed opportunity that's getting pretty old." The girls laughed and we went on to the next dream.

That little snippet, that event free dream, soon had us all on our feet cheering and congratulating the dreamer three weeks later. She had opened the drawers. They all held prison slacks, no underwear, no shirts, just prison slacks, blue with a white stripe down the side. There was one big difference. The material was a beautiful soft velvet. I remarked that it sounded as though something good was going to come from her prison experience.

"Wait, wait," she said waving her hands in the air. "It has! I was offered a job in the waste water plant. I didn't think I wanted to work there. It seemed a bad place to be, smelly! The person doing the job now gets out in August and they need a replacement. Then I remembered the dream, opening the drawers, looking at the opportunities, so I agreed to try it out. I actually like it!" We cheered.

"Wait! Wait! There's more," she said. "I can take courses and get a degree in wastewater management. I can get a job with a municipality!"

They all cheered. Words like steady income, benefits and taking care of herself were shared. There was recognition that we, the group, had witnessed another breakthrough.

I had been wanting to return to another woman whose dream the week before felt unfinished to me. I'd had further thoughts during the week. She was also feeling unfinished and jumped at the chance to work it one more time. Her dream had been about going up a set of stairs in front of a federal courthouse. Halfway up she is stopped by a man in a suit (a process server) who wanted to serve her papers. He said to her, "You will get five years in prison and four years' probation." She said, "I just served five years!"

The truth is she is five years into a ten-year sentence. There were things going on in the outside world for her that could have made this a predictive dream. We had no way of knowing at this time, so we continued to examine the dreams metaphoric possibilities.

Since we believe that all people and all objects can be parts of the dreamer, we took the image of the process server and worked that with the six magic questions. She described herself as the process server by saying she was a tall male, towering over her dream self. "I have dark hair, wear a blue suit with a gold badge on my right chest."

"As the process server, what is your purpose?" I asked her.

"My purpose is to deliver a message," she answered.

"What do you like about being that person?" I asked.

"I like the feeling of authority, of being the boss," was her reply.

"What don't you like about being the process server?" I asked.

"I don't like having to hurt someone." She answered.

"What is your biggest fear?" I asked.

She said, "Getting hurt myself."

"What is your greatest wish?" I finally asked.

"To retire. To not get involved with this anymore and to be safe," she answered.

When I asked where in her life some of these sentences applied, she saw a pattern. She saw how giving the message was the lying she'd been accused of doing for her boyfriend. Her offense was that the authorities accused her of having lied, twice, about whatever he did. She saw how it hurt her. She pretty much knew all these things. So, we turned to the image of the stairs that she stood on in the dream for possible answers. We did the six magic questions with herself being the stairs in the dream.

The phrase that slapped us in the face was given when she said she didn't like being those steps because they were black, shiny marble. Her greatest fear was that when it got mopped, she (as the stairs) would be very slippery, and people would get hurt because of her.

The beauty of the group showed through once again. They chided her about being slippery, sliding from boyfriend to boyfriend. She tried to help this boyfriend and got hurt herself.

She could bring this all into her current situation. If she were the process server, she would be trying to clean up a mess. Her desire was not to hurt or get hurt anymore. The group told her she needed to go slowly when the steps are wet! And now she knew what made her steps slippery, the wrong men. So profound!

Another woman had been reporting a series of dreams in which her boyfriend is giving her gifts. She told me from the second such dream that she had a boyfriend and a husband. The week before the boyfriend, in the dream, had given her a candle holder shaped like a clown. The clown's hands were held out in front to form a place for a candle. The candle didn't come with the gift.

Belonging to a man (or men) was her identify. Unfortunately, this was where she got her sense of self-worth. She seemed to have nothing else to hold onto.

This week, three Mexicans were chasing her, trying to kill her in her dream. "Honest," she said, "I have no prejudice. They are the old image of little men in big sombreros, serape, bandoleer filled with bullets slung across their chests in the shape of an X. I can't recall seeing any guns, but they wanted to kill me! I ran to my grandmother's house to hide. Peeping through a window, there, I soon saw them on the street. I then ran to the church. They broke in and found me there. They put a rope around my neck and just as they were to hang me a man in a brown suit said, 'Let her go! They did."

The other inmates had an immediate opinion. "Your three boyfriends!" they shouted out, much to her embarrassment. We tried to work her connection with Mexicans as a race, but she had no idea, no good and no bad ideas about them. It kind of boiled down to those bullets with no guns. They, like she, lacked the power to use what weapons they had. We also found it interesting that her savior was in the church.

We chose the Mexicans to work with the questions.

"Close your eyes and become one of those Mexican bandits" I directed her, "Describe yourself."

"I'm short and have a big mustache, my hat is black, and I wear a silver ring," she replied.

"What is your purpose?" I asked.

"I'm part of the crowd. I'm there to hurt people: she answered.

"What do you like about being the bandit?" I asked.

"I like belonging, having a purpose." was her answer.

"What do you not like about being a bandit?" I asked.

"I don't like having to hurt someone," she answered.

"What is your greatest fear?" I asked.

"Getting hurt myself. The man stopping me," was her answer.

"What would be your greatest wish as a bandit?" I asked.

"To be handed a job I can succeed at, to retire and not have to do this anymore." was her answer.

A lot of talk went back and forth about her misplaced trust in this group she was putting her faith in, the three boyfriends and her need to find another purpose in life. She was resistant. Her male friends were all she was interested in, all that made life seem real. I reminded her of the candle holder of last week. It was a gift from her boyfriend, shaped like a clown. The hands held out before it was waiting for a votive candle. I asked if she would mind returning to that character, be that character and work the six magic questions. That was okay with her. We started the questions, but she did not get very far before she erupted in a violent fashion. "He's making a fool of me!" she stormed. She finally got it!

The girls applauded! They pointed out to her that her whole demeanor changed in that moment. She went from being the cry baby 'woe is me person', 'why did they forget my birthday' person, the 'they'll get around to me sometime' person to a strong angry woman. She went from her usual moaning way of talking to a strong, indignant woman with whom no one was going to mess around. The other women pointed this out and helped rebuild her ego. She is better, stronger than she previously thought.

It was interesting, and I told her so later, that she found her salvation in a church. In the dream she took refuge in a church and the man in brown saved her from being hung in the church. She seems puzzled so I just asked her to think on it.

The next dreamer reported a dream that included her love of expensive toys.

"I drive up to my mother-in-law's house in my Corvette. I'm dressed in horse-riding clothes. I go inside to talk to my kids and while I'm there the cell phone rings three times. Then my ex comes in, grabs my wrist. I get away, run out and jump in my car and race all the way home. I go inside and am pushing the door closed when he puts his hand through the partially opened door and grabs my wrist again. I slap him and shut the door on him. He pushes it in and grabs my wrist again. I wake up with that feeling of a hand closed around my wrist."

She woke terrified. The fears returned as she told the story. It's amazing how real these episodes are in one's mind. These are the emotions with which God works. Perhaps the surface lesson, if she didn't already know it, was to stay away from this man and/or men like him. We returned to working the dream.

We picked up on the way she was initially dressed, and I learned she loved riding horses. She also loved Corvettes and had at some time, lots of toys. Well, those toys were not going to do her any good in the present situation. In the situation, in the dream, she got sidetracked. Her goal had been to visit with her kids. I asked her to look at her life and see where she might be sidetracked. This brought the usual guffaw and reminder from all, "We're in jail!"

I asked her to look at her life before prison and see where she'd put her life on hold. Where was the defining moment, the decision that took her off her path? I pointed out that, metaphorically, her ex was an ex-part of her. If she were the ex, what was it she was trying to tell herself about an old, perhaps forgotten, part of her?

I said that perhaps she is shutting a door when she really needs to see what is on the other side.

Our last dream was funny. Our dreamer was at the beach.

"There are two male friends about knee deep in the water when an old, wrinkled, toothless shark tries to attack one of them. I try to save my friend by distracting the shark. The shark stands up, about six feet tall, as it bounces about on its tail fins, stirring up the water. I laughed through the whole dream," our dreamer said. "Then the shark invites me to come home with him. 'My wife would like to meet you,' he said. I woke up laughing!"

What a picture, a toothless old shark. Since everything in the dream is the dreamer, she acknowledged her view of herself might be as a shark grown old. She also found herself to be harmless. When we began recognizing this that ah-ha look came into her eyes. She mentioned that she can find humor in most every situation and sometimes that irritates people. She's known for barking in the ear of whoever is ahead of her in line. Two of the inmates had shot her dirty looks the day before the dream because of her smiling so much; so she said.

"You're still stirring up the waters, doing what seems to you to be a harmless dance, I told her laughing. She agreed she probably did it on purpose.

CHAPTER SIX

My teaching tool this night never was used. I'd planned to talk about persona and how the clothes you wear in a dream, or the car you drive, say something about how you perceive yourself, consciously or subconsciously. Changing clothes in a dream is significant to changing the face you present to others in life – good or bad.

Instead, I squeezed in a plea to remember the source of these great messages we've been getting. It's not life repeated, it's not a TV show you saw the night before; it comes from deep inside you, from someone who cares about you and wants the best for you. And it only comes one step at a time. When you see you've improved your life and/or chances at life, you must watch your dreams for the next step. You'll get a different story line. You'll see where your attention now needs to be focused.

We jumped right into the first dream and sadly departed two hours later with the guard saying we'd stayed too long. There was just not enough time!

Our first dreamer ultimately shared four dreams that night. She was a perfect example of what I'd been saying, when you finally get the true message of the dream, the dreams will change. She was the one who, the week before, reported a breakthrough in dreams and life. She'd just taken a job in the prison in which she could get a degree and have a profession with benefits! Now her dreams were touching on other parts of her life. She told her dream. "I'm in a department store at the vanity counter looking at myself in the mirror. I'd just put on my favorite perfume, Heaven Sent. I thought it cost $15.00, but looking in the mirror I become confused, $25 or $51? It must have been the first amount, because I give the clerk a twenty and get change. Then I'm in a grocery store in the produce section. One of my fellow inmates comes in and barks like a dog in the ear of a teenage male. The boy turns to me and asks, 'What did she say?' I replied, 'I don't know." The inmate came back to buy something and was looking for her male ID.

"The scene shifts, (as dream scenes often do). Now I'm walking on the beach, I walk past a bar. A man calls to me, but I pretend not to hear him. I didn't hear him."

First, the number 15 appeared three times. 1+5=6. One girl remarked that it was the sign of the devil. Liking this dreamer very much, we all rejected that. I vowed to remember, next time, to tell them the Bible says, "All good comes from God."

The six we decided to look at as being more than halfway there or over the hump (10 being total and 5 halfway. The dreamer was battling an alcohol addiction; she was searching first in the department store vanity counter, next the grocery store produce department and lastly on the beach.

We noted that on the beach she finally turned her back on the bar and the man. She was over the hump. The water at the beach was also a reminder of her new wastewater job that was helping her over the hump. When she got out of prison she would be moving in with her elderly parents. Her life would become one of trips to the department store and the grocery store, taking care of their needs. In the dream, she was searching for her identify once more. The male ID she searched for talked of her need to be strong for her parents and ready to take the male role in matters of life for them. The incident of the barking inmate might be a reminder to enjoy life.

Her next dream had her children white water rafting while she observed them.

"A man appears and chases me home. All he wants is one of the six cigarettes I have hidden under a rocking char. I know I'll be safe if I give them away. There is a red Bic lighter there also. Then the dream switches to an oval prison compound, six stories high."

She came to the board and drew the compound. "I'm in a shower at the bottom end of the drawing. I see what appears to be balconies (4) per floor going up to the top. The strange thing about the balconies is that none had any railings."

Someone blurted out, "No boundaries." She agreed.

Because of the drawing and the cigarette dream, it became clear to me she also had a smoking problem and that she was seeing the inside of her lungs.

"Well!" I said, "I'm about to make it very easy for you to give up smoking right now! That's what you look like inside your lungs. Those balconies are growths due to smoking!" The groans that followed were almost funny to me, that I could be so brutal to this room full of probable smokers.

The collective meanings we gathered about the rest of the dream were a danger, as white-water rafting, and how her ill health would hurt her children. The man the girls dubbed the cigarette man, was the urge that was hard to overcome and her telling herself of the need to get rid of the cigarettes to save herself. Perhaps this repeated 6 is the devil, as suspected by some, who is continuing to tempt her even though she swore she'd quit three months ago. We noted danger, the tempting of fate, in putting one's fingers under the rungs of a rocking chair.

Someone else wisely remarked on the action of a rocking chair, back and forth, the way one rocks from one decision to another. This brought her to remark that it was probably more about her alcohol addiction.

I pointed out that in the dream she was in the shower which is cleansing. All her addictions had the possibility of being washed away, down the drain. There were no boundaries, nothing holding her back, if she made the right choices, otherwise, she'd always be in a prison of some kind. The dreamer knows which ideas hit home, they get the ah-ha feeling and she had a lot of them this night. Time will tell, but I often suggest that in times of decision and weakness, remember the dream!

We learn from each other's dreams. One very interesting insight came from the next dreamer.

"I'm in an office, looking through a window at new falling s snow that is covering everything. I put my hand on the window and the glass is cold. "My female boss asked, 'Why don't you go home?' I replied, I'll stay and work."

She told us she was very concerned about going out into the cold world when it was her time to leave the prison. She did not feel prepared to start a new life at fifty. Our interpretation was that she had things she needed to finish, to work on herself. I suggested she rely on her dreams to lead her in the right direction. We noted white (the snow) could signify purity. With a deeper spiritual dimension and with more faith and trust, she'd find the proper clothing to face that cold world. The others shouted out possibilities of things she might do to earn a living. We ended laughing about being a Walmart greeter and how that appeared to be a fun job for 'old' people.

Have I told you? It was a great group! I know nothing of why they were in prison. The dreams and I took them where they were in their hearts, right now, no past judgments. It was a privilege to be working with them. There was so much heart in that room.

The next dreamer was riding in a green SUV.

"I'm in the middle row of seats, my mother is driving. My two uncles are sitting in the back seat. I'm reading aloud some legal papers that I just opened. It is good news, and we are all happy."

Of course, they all hoped this was a prediction of good news. She made a big issue of the car being in three sections, so I drew three boxes, attached, in a row on the board. I put her in the middle seat or box, her mother in the front seat or right box and her uncles' names in the left or back seat. Not knowing if this would lead anywhere, I related how once, when doing dream work with another group, we found something similar to represent yesterday, today and tomorrow; past, present and future. In the dream, she was reading legal papers in the present.

Actually, she was doing more than reading legal papers; she was in prison living a legal proclamation, trying to file papers to shorten her stay.

In the interpretation of the dream, she would get out of prison sometime in the future and would then resume the duties and joys of being a mother. The color green of the car pointed to a healing, the green of fresh life in nature's plants. Asking about the personalities of the uncles, we learned they were both serious men, hardworking and still able to laugh. These things are part of her and would be there to back her up when she needed added strength.

The girls pointed out that the uncles 'had her back'. She agreed. We also pointed out that these traits she likes make her stronger than she thinks she is. This was our girl who the week before realized she was being made a fool of by her three men. This dream gave proof she'd made a giant step forward. To truly grasp the entire meaning of her dream, we would have to wait for life to catch up or for future dreams. Either way, it was a freeing of her spirit, and we hoped, the lady herself.

Another dream came from another inmate. It also held much promise.

"I'm at my mother-in-law's and grandmother-in-law's home.
They are giving me financial advice. Grandmother is also playing with the baby, when the baby begins projectile vomiting. I quickly scoop up the baby to rush her to the bathroom. Suddenly there is no bathroom. I look down in my arms and realized, no baby!

The scene shifted, (as dreams do) to being outside in the yard. There I'm the goalie in a game of soccer. I defended the goal against my two ex-husbands."

Many ideas were tossed around in these sessions and what I'm bringing you are only a few of the ideas brought forth. Eleven or more women in one small room can get quite chaotic with excited voices wanting their idea to be heard. Often, they astounded me with their insights. I'm sure what hit us all immediately, was the need to protect home (the goal) against her two husbands.

Then I saw the disappearing bathroom and pointed out that a bathroom is a place to get rid of wrong attitudes. Projectile vomiting could be viewed the same way. We concluded the wrong attitude was gone already and it happened by being willing to listen to the financial advice. It showed she was admitting she needed advice on some subject vital to her life. No baby could mean she'd done some growing up in that area. She took charge in trying to help the baby. She was defending her goal! This seems a pat on the back for her emotional and spiritual growth.

The last dream from this sixth session seems a prediction, we all hoped not. We found out the truth by acting it out and developed a new way to view things.

The dream was short, "I'm reading a newspaper about a sex offender being loose in my neighborhood. I immediately fear for the safety of my little girl. In the dream she is school age but, she's only three. I pick up the phone, call home to my mother and tell her of the sex offender.

I'll get right home, Mom, keep my baby there if she gets home before I do. I go to the school and find my baby gone. I go to my mother's home and still don't find my baby. My niece and brother are there, asleep on the couch and not worried about anything. My mother paces back and forth with worry."

Since this was a short dream, I introduced them to dream theater. There were just enough women to take all the parts. The dreamer played herself. Someone played a talking newspaper and shouted the headline into the dreamer's face. One played the baby and so on. We ran through the dream just as she's told it and then switched parts. Now our dreamer was the baby. After going through it one more time we switched parts again. This time the dreamer was the sex offender. As she assumed each part, things appeared she hadn't remembered. The baby was perfectly safe and happy. The sex offender was constantly on the back of whoever played the part of the dreamer. The sex offender was the woman's fears plaguing her. Throughout each rendition, the mother stood out as picking up that worry.

One woman remarked, "Didn't you say your mother had a heart attack recently?" The answer was yes.

Our dreamer now knew she had to contain her fears, somehow find a little faith. I told her that some people believe babies choose their parents and most babies survive anyway. The baby had her own path to walk and, as a mother, the best she could do in her situation was to send lots of love. The best lesson was to never get in a position like jail again.

That dream theater ended with the participants remarking on having goose bumps from the very beginning and,

I must admit, I felt it also. It was one thing to read something and quite another to have the newspaper stand in your face saying' "There is a sex offender loose in your neighborhood! You've got to protect yourself and your baby! Get home now!"

On their way out the door that evening, I told them to watch their dreams for flowers. I would be sending them a bunch for Mother's Day and the flower would be a secret.

CHAPTER SEVEN

Wow! Where do I start? The Mother's Day flowers were delivered to the women, as promised, in their dreams. Some of them received them and some did not. I had three flowers in mind: tulips, lilacs and forget-me-nots. As they filed in, two reported flowers, both varying bouquets of tulips. They were tickled to think they'd received my dream message. I was sorry that all the women had not received dream flowers. I explained that while I was sending my flowers, I kept seeing a field of wildflowers instead. I figured the wildflowers were them, my wild women.

One person came in later, threatening to get even with me as my flower gift had made her work harder than she ever had before. We laughed and asked her to hold the story till everyone got there. The last woman in the room reported she'd sent me flowers! She pulled out a photo she tried to send me and described it as a field of wildflowers with a beautiful rainbow over it. This was almost exactly the picture I'd told them had been blocking my efforts. They were all shocked, but I was pleased. Rainbows have special meaning to me.

One of the female guards had asked to sit in for a few minutes and caught this action so, by way of explanation to her, I drew Carl Jung's wave theory on the board. We, our conscious part, are each a tip of an iceberg riding in one of those waves in the ocean of humanity. All we are ever consciously aware of is contained in that tip of the iceberg that rides above the water line. Below this lies our subconscious; that part of us that holds all our memories and life happenings whether we remember them or not. Below that, deep in the sea is the part of us that is connected to everyone else. This explains how we touch each other in our dreams and where some of our dreams came from. There is more to it than that, but that was enough for the moment.

Our last class member to arrive had gone to sleep, accessed these deeper regions and sent me the image of a field of wildflowers. This explains some of our dreams that are of people we know. Perhaps something stressful is going on in their life. Usually, if you phone them, you'll find the dreams are like whatever is going on in their life.

The inmate with the grudge against my flower gift said that what I sent her was a huge bucket of white, self-rising flour. You might guess, she works in the prison kitchen, and she is the one who dreamed of the old toothless shark a couple of weeks ago. This bucket of flour was never ending in the dream, she proceeded to bake. She dipped out a huge can of flour, rolled, pounded, shaped and baked, turned to the can and it was full again!

She kept baking and the can kept refilling. We laughed it's like God's good, once you tap into it, it keeps flowing. This girl seems loaded with talent. She draws, bakes, and has music in her dreams and a wonderful source of humor. We must find a way to direct all this. Give our group enough time and the dreams will lead us there.

Our group member who seems to be making so much headway, beginning with buying Gucci bags, to clown candle holders, to Mexican outlaws, and finally, the breakthrough of believing she was being made a fool, had a disturbing dream to report. It was so like the old her, and unlike the new her, she wanted to be first to tell her dream.

In the dream, "I am visiting my mother-in-law's house. She's a nice person and I like talking to her. In walks my ex and his ex-girlfriend! I got angry! I beat him up and then attacked her and beat her up. Then the scene shifted. I'm in a hospital and I hear my mother's voice consoling me. She says 'That's okay. That's not who you are anymore. You're better than that now.

Then the scene shifts again and I'm to see three male doctors. One is white, one black and one Spanish. They are hot looking! I go into separate rooms to see each and flirt with each man."

This would be a good place to describe the procedure of dream work. If you do dream work by yourself, write it all out. Then circle or underline the actions or feelings and the people and objects. These are the key words.

Dream: I'm <u>visiting</u> my <u>mother-in-law</u>. There I see my <u>ex</u> and <u>his ex</u>-back together again. I fly into a <u>rage and attack and beat</u> them both. The scene shifts. I'm in a <u>hospital</u>. My <u>mother's voice consoles</u> me. <u>That's not you anymore. You're better than that.</u>' I flirt with <u>3 doctors,</u> white, black, and Spanish.

Draw lines connecting each of these to the margin. Every person and everything is a part of the dreamer. The nice mother-in-law is the dreamer. "Visiting" shows a temporary situation. The anger is a slip the dreamer might be tempted to make in the future. The two exes are part of the dreamer's past. If it were my dream, this would be talking of how angry I'll be if I allow myself to slip back to old ways! As mother says, "That's not me anymore." Mother is the dreamer's inner and higher self. "Hospital" indicates the dreamer is in a healing place. The doctors also indicate healing. Three being the sign of the Trinity, I take this message to come from a very high source.

The women chided her to set her sights for a man much higher, like a doctor who could provide her with those Gucci bags.

As you can see, we decided the two exes (her ex-boyfriend and his ex-girlfriend) were both symbols of who she used to be. Opportunities would come for her to slip back into her old mindset. She should remember her mother's words, "You're better than this!" The hospital told of healing which is coming or may be a clue as to her occupation when she gets out.

Our self-rising flour person told another dream. "I'm in front of a very shiny, black, electric grand piano. The top is up. I suppose it could reflect myself. I was too busy to notice. I moved a group of pictures aside to make room for the big vase of flowers I'm expecting for Mother's Day (that I never got because you sent me self-rising flour!) Then I got behind the piano to connect the wires. I'm back out in front and push a few keys and pedals. It was amazing what it could do. Then I notice the pictures are back where they began. I move them again. They mysteriously move back again."

This took quite a bit of discussion. Clearly she was making a connection, but not seeing herself as she is. The pictures moving reminded us of the old phrase, 'Got the picture?' She was having fun in the dream and looked forward to making music. Making a connection by pressing the keys and pedals were all in her control. This would take some more thought and perhaps a few more dreams to be a true story line and message. I saw a lot of potential but finding out exactly what that potential is may take a few more dreams.

She had another dream to tell. "Andy Selic, he's a friend from my past. His family owned a trash pick-up business. In the dream Andy was watching me pick roaches (marijuana stubs) from a beautiful emerald, green ashtray. I'm putting them in the trash. Andy says he wants them, so I picked them out of the trash and gave them to him. The smell on my fingers was horrible, strong."

This, I'm sorry to say, really stumped us. I'm seeing the dope and wondering if she's still doing it and trying desperately to find something positive out of it. Change. She, or someone, changed their mind and this made her handle the roaches twice. Perhaps a change was coming. I asked for three personality traits of Andy. None were good and when I asked if she could see any of them in herself she replied, "Absolutely not!"

On my way home that night I was able to make a connection. Because of the desperate circumstances of her life and the subject matter, I was overwhelmed. Driving home I saw a similarity between her dream and one reported in my group that meets on the outside and had been told just the week before. My friend had seen herself in a paper bag. With her in the bag were notes written on pieces of paper. She felt the papers portrayed old issues in her life. Her job was to sort through these and get rid of them as she was finally done with them. Bingo! Sorting through old issues and getting rid of them. I decided to go back to this prison dream next week with my new thoughts and see if they resonate with her. She was not playing with an old addiction, she was getting rid of them! Andy, being a male part of her needed to be healed. Her recoiling from him and all he represented shows she's well on the way to seeing how bad drugs are, the wrongness in doing this. The ashtray being green was also a sign of progress because green is a healing color. It being emerald green now makes me laugh. Perhaps it represents the Emerald City of Dorothy and the yellow brick road fame. Her little world is taking on a promising shape.

I would guess this person's inner view of herself is not very good. The dream used the trash man to portray what she thinks of herself. The week before, she was a wrinkled, old, toothless shark. There's hope. Now she's a shiny black electric piano, waiting to be played. This confirms my theory that who we are meant to be is programmed into us from before birth. Perhaps that beautiful emerald green ashtray will turn into a more useful bowl in the future.

One woman mentioned she'd be out in six weeks. It's probably time to talk to them about how things change for the good, how doors of opportunity open when you realize what the dreams are trying to tell you. Early on, in my dream work, I hesitated to say this. I didn't want people doing dream work just because they'd get a reward in this class. When they left me, I didn't want them to give up on this. There is always more.

There is another aspect. Our lady with a bright future, who opened the drawers of the antique dresser in her dreams, brought three new dreams. One step forward is good, but life is complicated. It always takes more than one thing to change. God leads us step by step.

Our 'Antique dresser' inmate dreamed she visited the music section of a pawn shop. "The owners are friends of mine. They need to leave for a short time and leave me in charge, they trust me. When they come back, they help me take three black folding chairs off the wall. The scene shifts. I'm in my high school music band room. There are three levels of risers with black music stands and no chairs. I'm on the top riser and very carefully step backwards, down the first, down the second, making my way to the conductor position. I've delivered my two children there to practice their lessons."

The music ties in with her love of playing the saxophone that she once did in high school. The dreams also show a responsibility to get the children to school to practice and a trust to get chairs for them. This is an important part of her life. All things and people in the dream are her. The missing conductor is her. She was heading toward that position. She had to watch where she stepped. There were all kinds of music stands that might trip her.

We are guessing that her life, after prison, is being rounded out for her. We talked of volunteer opportunities using music that she could immerse herself in after her 9-5 job. She is being warned of something that could trip her up, spoil her plans. The second dream made that clear.

In her second dream, "I'm a child, once more, with my whole family gathered around. My stepmother is disciplining me for something. I try to explain myself, but she doesn't let me talk. She takes out a gun and shoots a hole in my leg. I look down but there's no blood, just a hole. I look at my brother. He says 'She bought you a ticket. You are going away to marry a man she's chosen'."

The inmate continued, "I can't, I want to say that I need to go to work. I have responsibilities there. No words come out of my mouth. I wake feeling helpless."

To make a long story short, she figured out that if she told her plans of attaining a degree in wastewater management to anyone outside the prison, she'd be shooting herself in the leg. Her family probably does have plans for her. She would protect her plan and her strength by keeping her mouth shut. No words will come out of her mouth about this until it was all finished and the degree was in her hands.

CHAPTER EIGHT

Four women showed up for this week's session. Other meetings were occurring, so that kept our number low. This night a religious retreat is being held. The chaplain and other volunteers were attending.

In my meeting three women reported having dreams. I shared one of mine and we did a lot of talking. I found my personal philosophy meant as much as the discussion about dream content. Just like dream work, they listen and then take it or leave it. The discussion was uncensored and interesting. I found out what they thought.

In the first dream shared, our lady is in her sister's car. "My sister's boyfriend is there also. We go home. My sister dyes my hair and fixes it up nice. Then she and I go to the mall. At one point I have an armful of Bongo shorts and shirts. Then I see a jacket I like. I tell the clerk I'll give her $100.00 for the bunch. She hesitates so I add, 'It's summer, and you won't sell them now. Take it or leave it.' The clerk took it.

"Then we go to the Chicago airport to shop. I'm dressed in blue jeans, white top and red shoes."

This dream had an emphasis on changing clothes or her looks. Changing clothes in dreams often signifies changes in persona, or how one wants the world to view them – or how one views oneself.

I asked her, "How much longer will you be in prison?" She proudly said, "260 days!"

New clothes and a hairdo will certainly be in order. Also comes the question for this inmate, "How will people react to me? How do I present myself?" The airport symbolizes the freedom she can find, the far-flung places she can go, emotionally and physically. I asked her if the Chicago airport had special meaning for her and she explained it was on her way home. Her sister was taking care of everything for her, her children, her bills, anything she needed in prison. This is a part of her that will change. She will be taking charge of herself.

Someone noted the red, white and blue costume of the airport and remarked about the patriotic colors. She launched into her story which included being framed by some people in high places because she had gotten hold of some written information she should not have. It was already in the hands of the authorities, so we cautioned her not to get herself in more trouble and to stay out of the limelight. She needed to take care of number 1, herself. She agreed.

The next dream was from our joker in the dream group. Her subconscious produces the funniest images! In this dream she tells us, "I'm walking down a sidewalk in a neighborhood with Sally." Sally is another member of the group.

I'm writing the keywords and phrases on the blackboard. I stopped and asked her to give me three words describing Sally. This brought a bunch of laughs as Sally slides forward on her chair.

"She's adventurous, great sense of humor, and she's wild!" our dreamer says.

"Ha! That's all you!" Sally countered knowing I'd say these things were all part of the person who had the dream. The character in the dream (Sally) is used to bring out parts of the dreamer's personality.

Someone pointed out that the dreamer is beside herself and that truth about her life brought a lot more laughs. "But wait until you hear what she did!" the dreamer says. "Sally, in the dream, points out a black and white, long-haired cat that is wearing a dress. It walks like a person on its hind feet. Sally tells me to go get it! I hold back. We watch as the cat goes up a few steps to a fancy door and knocks. A Korean lady answers the door and lets the cat in. The cat goes down on all four feet to cross the threshold but stands up again and disappears down a hallway. The door closes and Sally tells me to follow the cat. I knock on the door and the same lady answers. I can now see the cat going down a hall and into a room. I follow. Inside the room is a younger Korean woman – 18 or 20 years old. She owns the cat and gives me an arrogant stare. Oh, I forgot to tell you, Sally has an arrogant stare!"

We asked her to take the role of the cat, "Describe yourself." I said.

"I've got long fur. I'm prissy and I'm royal."

"What don't you like about being that cat?" I asked.

"I don't like long hair!" Our dreamer answered, swishing her hair back and forth. "I'm going to cut it as soon as I get out and donate it to Locks of Love. I don't like wearing dresses!" They are all dressed in the prison skirt uniform today.

"What is your purpose as a cat?" I asked.

"To be warm and cuddly," she answered.

"What is your biggest fear being a cat?" I asked.

"Not being accepted," she answered."

"What is your biggest wish as the cat?" I asked.

"To get out of this dress!" she answered, to which they all laughed. If you could see this tall manly female, you'd understand.

"If it were my dream," I began, "it would be mirroring my frustration with my life as it is. The dream is offering me yet another image to have fun with, maybe once again pointing out a talent I have for comedy and telling me not to waste it."

I pulled out some one-panel cartoons I'd been saving for her. Her comment, the last time we talked of this, was frustration at drawing a series of panels and I wanted to show her a simpler way to do cartoons.

"Guess what!" she said. "One of the guards asked me to draw a cartoon for an important dinner they are having for another guard."

"You won't get in trouble for poking fun at them, will you?" I cautioned.

"Heck no!" she replied. "Everyone likes this guard that's retiring. I'm honored!"

As we went back to her cat dream, the girls thought it was referring to a certain Asian-looking inmate who was causing trouble for the dreamer and that would explain the Korean element. It's as if the cat was saying, "You hang with your kind, I'll hang with mine!" Another inmate added, "You can't win every time."

Dreams come on more than one level at a time. They can have more than one meaning. It's said that deciphering a dream is like peeling back the layers of an onion. We left it with the dreamer to pull back more layers and turned to the next person with a dream.

The third dream was short but powerful. "I'm walking toward a long driveway that leads to my childhood home. The large yard is filled with alligators of all sizes. A young boy stands about halfway up the driveway. The alligators put their mouths on him, but he was able to shake them off. I wanted to save him."

"Miss Carol, did this dream just come because I saw the news last night about the three people who died from alligator attacks?" she asked.

"The dreams use what you know to tell you what you don't know," I told her. "This news story just triggered something your psyche wanted you to think about."

We talked about her recent frustration with a group she had to meet with that was trying to help her grow emotionally. They had talked about selling drugs and why she'd done it. She got quite vocal, telling them she'd be lying if she said she didn't enjoy the money she made. She pointed out the need to support her brother and sister. She thought it would be lying to say the words they wanted to hear.

She also said her boyfriend wanted her to spend some time in the law library and see if there was any way she could get out earlier. She didn't want to do this. I suggested that the home she was trying to reach in the dream had a yard littered with things she didn't want to do; the words the teachers wanted to hear, and the paperwork required in trying to get an early release. These could be the alligators. They could also be lies she is telling herself. To work fully with God, you need to reach a place of humbleness, admit you don't know it all. Admitting these lies would help her reach that place.

The next week she didn't show up. She was in the 'Break Your Addiction' help class where they are forced to examine their motives and find out who they truly are. This prison is a great place to be, if you must be in prison, and I hoped she would have some revelations between their prodding and her dreams pushing. Other women had just finished this class and found it very helpful.

I said I'd had a dream of my own to work. It took place in an old bedroom that, besides being covered with a layer of dirt, appeared to be in a war zone. There was a bed in the middle and dressers were tipped over all around the walls. I used a strong vacuum cleaner with a hose attachment to suck up things behind the dressers. I couldn't see what I was sucking up and every few seconds something huge went up the hose. Someone said it was time to get the children's picture taken. What shall I dress them in, I wondered (still in the dream)? I know, I'll buy new clothes! The eight-year-old girl got a pretty red velvet dress.

The women asked me what I thought the meaning of my dream was. I replied that my work is to clean out the hidden corners of others' lives as the vacuum cleaner was doing in the room. One said there were a lot of mighty big issues I was sucking up. That's true. If so, this dream confirmed that I am doing the right thing. The red in the velvet dress is the passion I have for what I'm doing and my hope that some of my students would take on the persona of my work.

The one who hadn't shared a dream told how inmates in her compound, knowing she is taking this class, often seek her out for help with their dreams. She asks them how they feel about the characters, she does the six magic questions with them, and says "if it were my dream." She has been a good student and gets the red velvet dream dress.

This class will graduate in a few more weeks and I'll have a new group. The graduates will get a certificate. So cool! I'll miss them. God is good for leading me to this work.

CHAPTER NINE

There was a full house at the next session. We were all happy to be together again. Some of the inmates had been involved with the religious retreat last week. The girl with the alligator dream was in another class this evening, so I asked her friends to take her a message from me about the alligators blocking her path. Perhaps the alligators were symbolizing the people she reportedly disliked from another class, who were trying to convince her about things she denied. Another thought was that the paperwork for early release her boyfriend wanted her to work on was reflected in the alligators in her path or, perhaps the alligators were lies she was telling herself. I told them that to improve yourself you must start from a place of humbleness, admit you don't know everything.

The first dreamer had a nightmare where she and many others were being raped. She said, "This is the first time I've had such a dream. I know demons and evil beings walk the earth. I found it written in the Bible!"

"You don't have to let them into your life," I replied. We talked about a few ways trouble or devils get invited into your life; alcohol, drugs, being negative, gossiping, lying.

"Taken from a metaphoric point of view," I told them, "you have to look at your life and see where someone might be raping you, taking advantage of you. Or the dream could be an experience. Our bodies have needs and when we women are deprived for a time, dreams make it up. I believe the fear in the dream is your dread of the devils in life and the fear you were doing something wrong."

She was a little disappointed, I think. We told her that next time she dreams a similar dream to choose someone with whom she'd like to have sex. It was a rather rowdy discussion with hoots and hollers all around.

The next time I would ask her to think about the verse in the Bible, "Fear not, for God is with you." My dreams changed that verse around, long ago, to the words, "if you have fear, you don't have God." Powerful but true.

The next dreamer, our Joker in the group, had a novel dream. I'll try to condense it here. "It seems a replay of my life," she says, "except the ending is wonderful. I start outside a bar with my red pickup truck. I'm aiming to wash it. My feet are bare. I travel many places in this dream, meet several people from my past, meanwhile always trying to wash the truck. One guy finally washes it for me. I pass by a few more bars. In the last bar the prison chaplain is rehearsing a play on a stage. I want to be a part of it.

All the while I've walked barefoot everywhere, and I can't go in the bar because I'm barefoot. Another friend takes me to my home. I see a sick cat reaching out its injured front paw to me. I look at my own feet to see them covered with pennies that change into nickels, then dimes, then dollars."

I say "Wow! Money increasing at your feet! Your foundation is becoming more worthy."

Here are a few of the comments made during the discussion of this dream. We suggested she was not feeling acceptable to some section of society. She walked a strange path, but finally gets home. Don't we all go 'home' in the end? Someone does fulfill her greatest wish and cleans her truck. What is her greatest wish in life, to clean up her act? Perhaps it's to be acceptable in society? The cat is her sticking out her injured paw letting the world see her hurt. Her paws or feet are sprouting money. She has a profitable foundation.

The last bar where the chaplain was putting on a play, we believe, said something about the positive impact this chaplain is having on her. The bare feet said something about the nakedness of her soul. She is uncluttered, simple, there for everyone to see. This is one very interesting person. She was also glad to see that she was passing up the bars! We encouraged her to work on her cartooning. No one has had the amazingly funny images she has.

The next dreamer met her boyfriend on the street of a dark city. "He gives me a gun that I tuck into my hooded jacket and then he disappears. I start walking. Suddenly cops are everywhere shining enough lights to make the city bright, but they don't see me. I get to a corner and run smack into a detective. She asks me if I've seen _____? I say no. Then the scene shifts, I'm in a restaurant where I'm joined by two people for dinner. They break into a big argument and one of the two people changes into a monster, getting uglier by the minute. I run to the bathroom to hide. The monster chases me to the bathroom."

This dreamer was extremely grateful for the dream interpretation, because she was afraid of being drawn back into the old life, as if this dream was a prediction. After listening to the others, I was able to put together this: the cops are authority figures. God is an authority figure. He shines his light to make us aware, heal us, to bring us into His holy awareness. The gun is her power which she is keeping hidden. Her power is what she came into this world as a baby to do. The monster is the part of her that holds this power (or secret) and the monster is getting anxious to bring it out into the open. The bathroom is the place of eliminations, of getting rid of false or wrong attitudes.

The last dream we did was from a person who'd made a huge change to her life in the ten weeks we'd been doing dream work. Her future was looking good in many ways. The last dream she reported emphasized her addictions. This one is talking about another area of her life, her ex-husband. She explained they'd been separated for a while before her arrest. They both had drug problems.

"In my dream," she said, "I'm back home with Bill. We get a DVD from the video store and head home to watch it. There is an address label on it with the name Joe Braso. The name sounds familiar, but I can't recall anyone by that name. I don't know why it would be in my dreams. When I put it into the DVD player Bill wants to have sex and I say no. I want children but I don't want to have sex to get them. I think a minute and say I'll do artificial insemination. In life I'm concerned about my brother and his wife not getting pregnant, but that thought didn't come to me in the dream. I'm given two sperm, a girl and a boy and as I look at myself, I can see them swimming around inside my stomach."

I pick up on something right away. I inform her, "The DVDs are old memories, ready for replay, and if you want to go back to your husband it would be replaying the past, maybe stepping back into the same problems. It might be artificial as in artificial insemination."

"You're right," she said. "I know that on one level, on another I don't know it and I'd been thinking about him lately. This message is clear about it though. Guess this isn't about my brother."

"Dreams come on more than one level, this may also be about your brother." I paused. "That name, wouldn't it be wild if you sit down for a divorce and he's the judge?"

We only had ten minutes left, time goes so fast doing dreams. I rewrote one of the short dreams on the board and showed them how their journals should look. "Circle the people. Underline the things, feelings and places, numbers and colors. Draw lines from them to the side and do word association.

"Think on each item separately. See how many things you can get out of it. This will help you decipher your dreams, but it's best to share it with someone else. Ask their opinion."

We only had one more session to go. I wanted to make sure they had all the tools I could give them. The week after would bring a whole new group of women.

One of my wild women shows me a picture of her eighty-year-old grandmother. They talk and write a couple of times a week. Grandmother is as excited about the dream class as my student is and gets copies of all the handouts. The women are all so neat! This work validates me like nothing has ever done before.

CHAPTER TEN

The last meeting of the twelve-week session with the first group went so fast my usual note taking didn't happen. The possibility of seeing them again to report on any insights I might have had afterward were remote anyway. The meeting went fast with many dreams to tackle. There were a few things left unsaid. I hoped they do dream work and could pop into class once in a while as they had promised.

It would have been nice if I could have come up with a mentor for our Joker who has access to this world of cartoons and/or ideas for cartoonists. I attended an orientation meeting for new volunteers and while many people were there to do church services, a few were there to mentor. The mentoring was what was needed. A mentor that would continue with an inmate after she was out of prison, helping her to not let things return to the same old world she knew before.

One person I'd like to have had a chance to get back to was the lady who had the demons in the first meeting. She got rid of the demons and went on to sex dreams. She said that she thought of herself as a pervert. I needed a chance to help her get beyond this. She learned that her sex dreams were not uncommon and felt better about herself, but I wanted to shake her up a little. To me, she was wasting a lot of precious dream time that could be used to find out why God put her here. She could find direction for that day she would get released and had to fend for herself. I vowed to try to get word to her somehow.

The first meeting with the new women was strange, but promising. Twelve were signed up, but only six attended. Strange. In the last class the women all knew each other. These didn't seem to know each other and, worst yet didn't seem to want to know each other. They spread out across the room, making it hard to talk to them as a group and they refused to move closer to each other.

Two women from the first class came. The Joker was one of them. Now, thanks to the dream group, she had friends. While we had come to appreciate her, she still talked about problems she has with other people. Her non-stop sense of humor consisted of barking like a dog in the ears of the person in front of her while waiting in line. Some inmates couldn't even entertain the thought of a smile.

I gave a little of my background with dream work and explained the process of working dreams in a group and/or by oneself. I first asked who would like to share a dream. As one person told a dream, I put the key words on the board. We asked questions about the dream, then we did word association, and finally we went into the "If it were my dream." phase.

Two of the six sat by themselves and talked in low tones constantly. I kept directing questions to them. I included them directly in my tales, but it was difficult.

The first inmate shared this dream. "I think I must have been on work release. I'm dropped off in an area of houses. I must get through the houses, across a field of mud to get to my red pickup truck. I know I need to be back at 6 PM or I'll be in violation and will have to go back to prison.

"I see an opening between the houses and go that way. I reach a hill and start going up. I'm traveling through deep mud that is getting thicker and I get stuck more with each step. Just as I'm about to give up I see a dark shadow of a person coming down the hill to help me."

"Let's take the words first," I said, "Take houses." I wrote on the board various metaphors like protection, safety, privacy, your life.

She points out, "None of the houses are mine."

"Perhaps you are looking at how other people live their lives," I said.

"That's the truth," she said.

I had to giggle. "If you're looking for that red pickup truck, ask _____."

Joker yelled out, "I got it!"

Then we took turns sharing Joker's dream and shared a laugh. I gave her an update. The truck in her former dream is her and she's been trying to clean up. She agreed.

"She was trying to come clean. You also seem to be a little lost," I said. She agreed.

Back in the new dream' "The need to get back before a certain time shows a sense of responsibility. If it were my dream, being dropped off is an opportunity for freedom but, in reclaiming my old life, (the red truck), my passion (red) my work (truck) I become stuck once again in old habits (mud). I'm going to need more help and that shadow of a figure is sent from higher up, from God, to guide me."

She like all. She said that, "Understanding it like that gives me a better feeling."

The next inmate gave a dream that we all entered into. "I'm driving up the driveway to the house my husband and I used to own before we got divorced and lost it. That was the best time of my life except we divorced before I landed in jail. In the dream, the house is still mine and I've come to reclaim it. It looks the same on the outside, but the inside has been gutted. There are no walls remaining. Someone, I don't know who, helps me to start rebuilding the inner walls. A lot of my things are still there, china, other things that were important to me. I could look out the windows and everything seems the same outside."

"I see the house as you changing inside." I said. "You look the same on the outside but there is a lot of renovation, remodeling going on inside."

"That's for sure," she said.

"If it were my dream," one of the women spoke up, "the broken insides would speak of my broken heart." Wow!

I thanked her and continued, "The china and things left from the past that were precious are the good memories that you'll always have no matter what."

Another woman spoke up, "If it were my dream, I'm looking at all that empty space and at the fun I can have building it the way I want and filling it with new, better things!"

This had suddenly turned into another group.

A third lady had her hand up for a dream, but I motioned her to wait while I walked over to our two whisperers and asked for a dream.

"Mine are all the same," said one. "I relive my crime, only it's being done to me. There's a person in this prison, in my own cell block who reminds me of my victim. I got bad vibes the first day I saw her," she added.

"How long ago did you commit this crime?" I asked.

"Three years ago," she said.

"Don't you think you can move on a bit, at least in your dreams?" I asked.

"Not as long as I have to see her," was the reply.

"Dreams use something you know to tell you something you don't know. If you can bring one of those dreams in, perhaps we can find another meaning to the dream and relieve you, somewhat of that scenario. I bet your relations with this person are zero." I said.

"I'm afraid of her!" she replied, trying to close the subject.

In <u>Where People Fly and Water Runs Uphill</u> by Jeremy Taylor, the author tells of a similar situation when he worked in a black district of Alabama. His fellow white workers were ineffective with the population they were trying to help. Built into their unconscious were fears that had nothing to do with the black people yet were portrayed in their dreams as black people. Jeremy found this out after resorting to dream discussion to fill their mandatory office time.

The attitudes of the men changed toward the ones they were trying to help, and progress began. Suddenly the residents began turning to them with trust and faith. That is a lot like projection. We dislike in others what we try to keep buried inside ourselves. Once we admit we have those tendencies also, we can see a reason why they act the way they do, the 'thing' doesn't bother us anymore.

I suggested that she needed to talk to this person.

"Not me!" She was truly afraid, and I wondered what she had done. Sometimes it is better not to know.

I asked the second whisperer to share, but she declines saying she wasn't thinking straight. One of my old timers explained how she knew this person had been up since four AM because she was working in the kitchen. Our whisperer said the next week she's has the day off and would be better able to be civil.

So, I returned to the lady on hold.

"There had been a flood and I'm standing on an island. There are two ways off this island. One is a strong, solid concrete bridge. This other is a swinging-rope bridge. The rope bridge goes into the dark murky water where there is a strong undertow. It would be very dangerous to cross that way but that is the way I go," she tells the dream group. "I figure I know what it means, I've always been an adrenaline junkie and always took the dangerous route. That's why I landed in here."

I asked her to come up to the board and draw the island and bridges.

"Could be you're right," I said. "The concrete foot bridge is the straight and narrow and it's higher than the rope bridge."

"I hope, after all this, I can be content to take the high road," she said.

I remarked that finding her talents, through the dream work, and putting them to work in her life can be a much greater adrenaline rush.

"We'll have to wait for more dreams from you," I said, "You may be crossing that bridge by understanding your dream. I imagine more direction is coming. Dream work is an ongoing thing. Some people have come to my other group once or twice, found the answer to their immediate problem and not come back. Others have been with me more than two years. We need this guidance throughout all our lives."

CHAPTER ELEVEN

"I'm standing near a man who speaks strangely. I ask where he's from and he says Russia. We talk briefly. We watch as a bomb lifts off and shoots to the sky."

This dreamer woke from this dream very much afraid, literally shaking, that she'd been given a prediction. It seems that the outside news is a big thing in prison. As the inmates meet going from work to class, food, pharmacy, etc. they often greet each other with the latest they heard. This week the Koreans had shot off some missiles.

"They fell in the ocean,"I tell them.

The reply I got back had something to do with polluting the ocean waters.

Israel and the Hezbollah had just begun their fighting in Lebanon. It struck me as odd, this worry the inmates had, considering who and where they were. They are safer inside these walls than outside should anything disastrous occur close to us. Safer than myself during a hurricane. I pride myself on not judging so I let it go. I certainly didn't want to make them glad they were in prison. One big, universal worry they seem to have is their families.

"Let's try to find some metaphors in this dream," I said. "What do you think of Russian people?"

"They're people a lot like us," was the reply.

"The bomb?" I ask.

"That scares me. What does it mean? She asks me.

"When it explodes there'll be change, change coming in you. Maybe it is significant that it's taking off into the sky. It's like you have high potential," I said.

One of the other women answered, "Maybe it's the rocket NASA just sent off."

"Space exploration has become a joint effort between the US and the Russians. Maybe your future holds a joint effort with someone you might not have considered before. That Russian is also you, a part of you so far not recognized. If this were my dream," I said, "I'd be happy to have this dream. It may be talking about my being ready for great change in my life. It is bringing in a part of me no one knows, so far."

"I rarely get a prediction anymore," I felt a need to explain predictions. "Early in my recording of dreams I received many predictions. It can get boring writing down dreams you don't understand, and I felt the predictions came to keep me interested in the whole process.

"Actually, there is a belief in some circles that everything that happens in life happens first in your dreams. That explains déjà vu. So, you may well have been seeing some of what was going on in the world this week. I hope you've written this dream down. It will be interesting to see what comes next in life and in your dreams. If it was something in your life, I find dreams quite often exaggerate. Rather than reaching for the sky, you may get a new hairdo that gives you a great feeling about yourself, for instance."

"Not likely in here!" They all laughed.

A hand went up. "I have a recurring dream I don't understand," she said. "Steve, my boyfriend for the last three years before coming to prison is always in it. I'm looking for him. Each place I look he's just been there and gone. I can't seem to catch up to him. In the dream I miss him. Then I see him, but he shuts the door between us. In life I want nothing to do with him. It scares me to think I'd look for him anywhere. Why in my dreams?"

"Can you give me three words to describe Steve's personality?" I asked. That question always brings hoots and snide remarks. The other women have already heard about the bum.

"He's abusive and he's controlling. I was like his slave – the way he ordered me around, beat me, and expected me to get him money," she said.

"Everything and everyone in a dream is a part of you," I said. "This part of yourself has not been nice to you. You've not been nice to you. Dreams come on more than one level. While this dream is reinforcing you're not wanting to have any future contact with him, it also is telling you to look and nurture the good in yourself. Let go of the old ways." Being a new group, the group aspect had not fully developed yet so I did the talking. I find that when I take the first step, the others can and do come up with suggestions of their own.

Another said, "It's good that door is closed! That's not you!"

One of the two women who'd been busy whispering chimed in, "If he were my boyfriend, he'd be a dead boyfriend! You stand your ground, girl! He'd never last three years with me! That's your fault."

She replied, "I know. I'll never let anyone treat me that way again!"

It was only the second meeting, and they were bonding. Everybody was totally involved this week.

Our whisperer decided she'd share a dream. "I want to make this perfectly clear; I'm not this way in life. This is a dream! I got a husband! In the dreams I'm with four women I know, and they are acting like lesbians. I want to be their friend, like sisters, but they got their own plans. Biggest trouble in the dream is they fight over me, get jealous of each other. One of the four is better. In life I like her best, but she's playing with my emotions, too. I don't want any of that stuff. I don't like the controversy and I feel frustrated at trying to stop it. Then my Mom comes and says, 'You can't do that anymore. You must forgive yourself. Be still and be patient'. That's the end of the dream. I'm not that way but I've had the dream a few times."

In the course of the conversation, it came out that she'd seen herself as a tough guy. Nobody made her do anything she didn't want to do. I pointed out this may be the subject of the dream. Here, again, all the characters are her. She is struggling with aspects of herself she no longer likes.

One of the other women pointed out, "Life is sure different for you here. Everything is planned for you, and you obey!"

She agreed.

"Whenever words come in a dream," I said, "whether it's from my dead Mom or anyone, I pay close attention to the words. The words Mom says are good advice. It's a good feeling to know she's still with you, isn't it?"

She nodded yes. "She died right after I got in prison. I couldn't go see her when she was sick. Couldn't go to the funeral." She was clearly upset about this.

"That makes it even more special that she comes in your dreams and tries to guide you," I said. "I sat next to a woman in a meeting this week who wanted to tell me about her dream experience of the night before. Her husband died nine years ago, and he finally came to her in a dream. She said they had a great time talking over the good parts of their life together and talking about what he was doing now. She was so happy! This is real! God made a very complicated world and we're just seeing the tip of how things really are."

CHAPTER TWELVE

Halfway into the hurricane season, getting into prison had been difficult. When there is thunder and lightning, the prison goes into lock-down. The women are in their compounds for their own safety.

In Florida during the hurricane season, it rains every afternoon so there were not many opportunities for classes. One night (class time was from 6 PM to 8 PM) I went over just in case they would let me in. The storm was a long way off. They turned me away. Two other volunteers were standing nearby, and I heard one remark that we wouldn't want to be stuck inside if the electricity went off. It might take hours to restore the power and we wouldn't have a bed! How true. Better out than in.

Tropical storm Ernesto finally passed, and I was able to resume class. This second group had been down to three people but tonight three from the old group joined us and two new people. We would be starting a new class in two weeks and the new members wanted to try the class out before it officially started. We had a great two hours. There were several revelations in how the women viewed themselves.

The first dream reported was, "I'm home where I grew up. I'm sitting with a bunch of old friends in the dark around a campfire. Fish jump in the water near us. Frogs leap and splash and make frog noises. We reminisce about pranks we've pulled, trouble we've gotten into. It's time to leave and I get into a car with three strange people. They never acknowledge me. They seem more like crash dummies. The dome light is not bright enough to illuminate them. The car starts up, but drives backwards, faster and faster. I try to get out, but the doors and windows disappeared. I shout 'God! Stop this car now! Get me out!"

We all congratulated her on turning to God for help. As the old saying goes, there are no atheists in the foxhole, and this surely seemed like a foxhole situation to us.

We all long for home. Reminiscing could be a way of bringing up old issues like the pranks that are no longer acceptable. The fire is purifying, the water, fish and frogs are a return to doing what comes naturally.

Then, she recalled that two days after the dream, she had a visit from an old friend, and they did a lot of talking of the past. This dream could well have been a foreshadowing of this event. It is said that we live everything in life in our dreams before it happens in life. That's why sometimes we feel we've been there before, déjà vu.

Without knowing the rules, the new women picked up on the point that the car was going backwards. No good! Is there somewhere in her life where she may not be moving forward? She declined to answer. The zombie-like people are parts of her that want to be known. There seems to be no way out of this car. The car has become her prison. The positive aspect is that she is putting it in God's hands. In His timing things will work out.

Next, we turned to one of the new people. Her dream had happened several years ago. She'd already done twenty years of a thirty-year sentence. Around the time of the dream, she'd been into pentagrams and witchcraft that a group of prisoners were using to bring about a large drug deal in prison. Before it happened, she had doubts about who her higher power really was and if she was getting the right spiritual guidance. She went to sleep that night and asked, "Who is my higher power."

Her dream that night led her to step away from the witchcraft, step away from the drug deal and the prison friends. It led her to forget about the cement blocks she's chiseled out for an escape. Shortly after the dream, her good behavior was rewarded by going to a safer prison.

Her dream; "I'm in a penitentiary in the southwest. I see desert and mountains in the distance. I'm behind a high barbed wire fence and I feel like I'm being punished. A guard watches me while I break up large rocks, dig a trench and bury the debris. He goes inside to get out of the heat. It is hot! I feel someone staring at me and look around. I see nothing but mountains off in the distance and go back to work. I feel it again and look again. The third time this happens, I see an Indian man come down out of the mountains. He holds my eyes as he walks through the fence as though he's a spirit. The ground moves. He stops ten feet in front of me and motions for me to look behind me. A sleek, shiny black panther is standing there watching me also. His eyes are just like mine. The Indian says, "We are your higher power and are with you always. Before you came to earth you were with God.'"

Can't get more powerful than that! She said she had Indian looking siblings. The fact that the two spirits (Indian and panther) moved through the fence showed how she had no boundaries on what her soul could do. Being in prison did not limit her soul. This was confirmed by the guard going away.

I told her of being at the International Dream Conference this year and about the seventeen countries that were represented. One speaker spoke about making your heritage\culture a priority. It seems her dream came to teach her that. She instinctively turned to God through her guides and turned her back on the other beliefs. This was a major turning point in her life and the rewards came soon after, in the first part of the dream, her past or current situation, the breaking of rocks was showing her how she was just digging herself into a deeper hole.

The same night another woman described her dream as nothing but a snippet. It is surprising what a group can do with one little image. "I'm in a camping trailer, my whole family is gathered round. My mother-in-law brings me a beautiful fern. My husband comes in the camper to change his clothes."

Putting the dream on the board I circled the main words. I circled camper, fern, mother-in-law, husband and changing clothes. The camper, we agreed was a temporary situation. Then I asked her to give me three words to describe her mother-in-law. She said, "Leader, responsible, hardworking, the glue that holds things together." I told her she has just described herself. She has these traits inside herself. Everything and everyone in the dream is the dreamer.

"What about the fern?" she asked.

"Let's get some ideas from the group," I said.

The group responds with, "Green or healthy, fresh, growing, brings oxygen to a room, delicate." We addressed growing. Something was growing inside her of which she does not yet see; like the attributes she gave to her mother-in-law.

"What about my husband?" she asks "I want no part of him. He put me into slavery. He was nothing more than a pimp!"

My answer was, "He's changing his clothes. Not him in life, but him that is a part of you. You are changing your persona, your clothes, how people will think of you. It's all the work you are doing on yourself while here in these programs."

"It's best if you don't go home!" someone shouted out.

"I hope I don't," she replied.

The dream of changes, her clothes, and her persona was interesting, pointing out her good qualities and how she's been growing. The week before, she had told a different dream:

"I drive up to a crack house where my husband has left our children. I climb down from a pickup truck with high tires and go down into the building. I gather my children and send them out before I sit down at the table. I see a mirror with crack on it. I pick up the mirror, pass it to another person and leave, climbing back up into my tall pickup truck."

Her own interpretation, and we all agreed, was that she was over the hump of her addiction. She felt extremely good, knowing this was behind her forever. The high tires on her truck pointed out her higher view of life.

The last dream reported was from the other newcomer. To me, it was the story of how ill prepared some of us are for life and the story of the Phoenix raising from the ashes.

"I was actually six months pregnant when I had this dream. In the dream, I steal my husband's truck, but I don't know how to drive it. I shift into drive and try to coordinate my feet on the clutch and the gas pedals. I can't do it. The truck chugs, chugs, chugs down the street slamming me against the seat each time. Then it runs out of gas. Still in the dream, my husband wakes up and begins chasing me. I get out of the truck, grab up child after child after child, hold them to my chest and try to run with them. We're on top of a mountain and I'm at the edge of a cliff. I check to see if I have all the children, but when I take a good look, they've vanished. My husband turns into my angry father, I jump off the cliff. Next thing I'm floating above my body that is laying at the bottom of the cliff."

"If it were my dream," I sometimes put out a suggestion to get the others thinking and participating, especially after a traumatic dream like this, "the ride in the truck is symbolic of my start and stop life. It's symbolic of how I don't really know how to live it properly." She agrees.

"My husband chases me, but he's not my husband, he's symbolic of a part of me that wants me to turn and face it. I need to face up to something, maybe admit I need help." All were silent.

I continued, "The children could be my love of children (she nodded her head yes to this) and may be the direction I need to look for a financial future, teaching, nurturing, be an advocate of some kind. Another way to view it, we all have an inner child. Perhaps yours is fragmented and you were trying to pull yourself together."

They all gasped at this and said things like, "This is why I like this course." I had hit a truth for all of them. We can learn from others' dreams as well as our own.

"As far as the ending, you need to die to be reborn into something better. As Jeremy Taylor said, and I've quoted him before, "The little girl who can't tie her shoes has to die to make way for the little girl who can tie her shoes." When she had this dream, even though it came before she went to prison, a change was in the works. Perhaps she needed the lessons a stay in prison would bring. In spirit we are perfect, complete and must work to that goal in life.

Joker, you've read of her before, has made a breakthrough. She's the one who dreamed of a toothless, wrinkled shark, treading water by standing on its tail and swishing the water to stay upright. She also had the cat in a dress. The most serious dream she had was of picking marijuana butts out of a green ashtray. The humor in it was the violent reaction she had to the man in that dream. She'd never be like that!"

Her new dreams, two to be exact, were long stories. The lines of the stories alternated between things that would be good in society and bad in society's view. We decided she also felt that she's not yet made an internal commitment to improve her life.

With one dream on the board, I found myself trying to force an issue by erasing all the seemingly bad things, then remembered I was not to judge. I told her to ignore my ideas as it was her life. I did not want to interfere with her sense of humor, for one thing, as that truly came from her soul level and needed to be built and used rather than stifled. She needed to make the choices, when it was time to make them. Her sense of humor – it was part of her.

Perhaps she could build on it by pursuing cartoons. Her other dream was different (we probably hit a truth last time). "I am working outside the main gate with Bobbie. There is a nice garden there that we inmates maintain. All the people coming into the prison walk by it. We get a chance to do inspirational, patriotic, humorous and just plain pretty plantings there. I used to work in a garden at another prison. It was a high bank or berm. In my dream I'm trying to do a meaningful arrangement with flowers and bushes. All of a sudden, I notice I am not in my uniform but have on blue jeans. Bobbie said, 'You're not in uniform. You'd better change!' I reply, 'I don't care.'"

In our interpretation discussion, we said she was building a grand entrance to part of her life. She was building something that was inspirational and enlightening as though she had it in her to become a beacon or welcoming gate.

I asked her if she felt as though she'd finally made a commitment to do better with her life and she said she had. She went on to tell us of a time in her life when she worked in such a garden. She had taken a leadership role with her fellow inmates who also worked the garden, because she had great ideas. She talked of the creative enjoyment she discovered in herself. She described plantings she did for each holiday and happening. The warden often took pictures. Once a baby was expected to be born in the prison. At a loss for what to plant, she did three simple question marks. This meant different things to each person who passed but those who knew who the father was got a chuckle.

She said she felt she would channel her creativeness in the future in this direction. Someone in the group suggested she put her ideas into a book to sell to landscapers, apartment managers and housing developments – anyone doing gardens that made a statement for Christmas, Easter, Black History Month, etc. As she also liked to draw, this really seemed a possibility. It would channel creative juices in a direction that might help keep her away from the "good old" (bad girl) days.

One inmate reported this amazing dream that we tried to decipher until she told us the truth behind it.

"I sit in a restaurant with my father. He has a lottery ticket and he's just found out it is a winner. He wants to hide it. My step-dad comes in and they kiss each other. The truth is out of the closet. They are both gay. I leave and enter a black limo. The driver turns around. I don't recognize him. From the radio we hear that ____ ____ (my father) won the lottery and can collect if his daughter, ____ (me) let's him.

The scene shifts and I'm outside the car, watching the limo guy move firearms around in the trunk. As he takes out a gun, a knife, a big ax, I'm afraid he's going to kill me. Someone's going to get killed. Can you guess what this means?" she asked.

We tossed around a couple of ideas until she pulled out a letter from her step-mother. It told of the death of her father and step-mother's marriage. The letter suggested the reason for the divorce was that the lottery winning they'd been using for expenses was gone. Our girl said she never knew about that. The letter was so very much like the steps of the dream, we had to leave it there. Our dreamer had the dream one week before the letter reached her, about the time it was being written. You still think we are not connected?

CHAPTER THIRTEEN

This is the second night with my third group; there were eight students tonight and we had a good meeting. I passed out my favorite Bob Hoss Color Chart. On the back I had placed some Jungian terms that are helpful when studying one's dreams.

We talked about the Animus (he) in all females' dreams. He being our opposite who comes to show us the way. Sometimes it's a wise old man, or a youngster, or a man we know. I always stop and ask myself why that man and not another man I've met in life. There is a message attached to this person, a message that relates to the dreamer. The Anima (she) is true for men. She being a goddess, a flirt, a co-worker, someone we went to grade school with. What about this person can possibly be within the male dreamer?

We also talked of the role of the ego and how much more there is in us that we try not to see. Against the wishes of the ego, these things work their way to the surface. These are often feelings or emotions; complexes we've consciously buried from our past. They can be a feeling of guilt we must deal with, or they can be a talent we've not acknowledged. So, these things we try not to see can be good or bad. They hold lessons for us.

If you want to know where to find more information on these topics research Jungian Psychology.

The first dream of this class was from a person who was getting cold feet about being set free after twenty years in prison. In the dreams, "I am in a small business and go to change its filters.

(Volunteers have found a McDonalds job for her. She needs to stay in this area for eight months.) I found the filters were all gone. I'm determined to find a way to make a filter. I look and find a large sponge that I can use. It has two colors, pearly white with one small black speck on one side and a beautiful soft blue on the other. Don't know if it's been used before as the black spot might suggest. I try to remove the black spot but can't. I cut the sponge in two and use the white half as a filter."

As I wrote the keywords on the board, we tried to do word associations. Filters keep out the bad or unnecessary. Filters protect! Filters are a necessary part of a lot of things.

The word 'change' was significant as a big change was coming in her life. She talked of the pros and cons on her choice of where to move when she finished her time. She wondered whether her mother will be able to move with her or maybe she should try to stay near her mother. She got into trouble in that area before but felt stronger about herself after serving her prison time. We pointed out she was filtering through a lot of information, a lot of decisions.

She used the white side of the sponge – white being purity or sacredness. It may be, to her, the little speck of black was her crime and jail time, or even her new use of her unconscious through dream work. She said she was asking God each night to guide her in making these decisions. She would live by that decision when it came.

Many things were clear. She had a bright mind, a can-do attitude (making a filter out of a sponge) and was confident, a much-needed attitude. Confidence would also save her from disappointment should the promised help not arrive as expected.

Another interesting dream came from another inmate. The variety of images from these women astounded me. She told us, "Two friends and I are building two rooms. The first room has a floor that we neglected to attach to the walls, and it tips as we walk across it, sinks low when we are near the edge. I pull up the carpet and see a comforter folded up underneath. We cross a walkway to the other room. There the floor is solid. There's little furniture in the room, a bed and chair and a grey Jeep."

I began the discussion. "If it were my dream, crossing the walkway would show a significant shift in my thinking." The hands went up.

"The unstable floor, the rocky floor, if it were my dream, shows how I've been thinking" one woman said. "The solid floor shows where I'm going or where I am now!"

"Good thoughts and along the line of my own," I said, "The comforter brings to my mind how some people, on their death beds hang onto life even with its pain, because they are afraid of the unknown ahead. If it were my dream, I'm hanging onto my old ways because it's something I know."

Another hand went up. This inmate added, "Maybe it's saying that comfort landed her in jail and it's best to bury it now." Another woman pointed out the stability of the new room and declared this a positive dream pointing out the change that was happening in the dreamer's heart. The bare room was what she had to start with and that's good, because she could now fill it with good things.

"I used to drive a grey Jeep," the dreamer said.

"The car of my dreams," I pointed out, "for a long time, was a humble Volkswagen bug. I believed, at the time, it was saying something about how I saw myself; humble is how you must be to approach God. Everyone here is humble in that you are taking this class. You admit you don't have the answers.

"If I saw myself as a Jeep, to me the Jeep is a workhorse, dependable, goes over rocks and places no other car will go. I think that's a good thing." The dreamer was smiling and thoughtful. She now had a lot to think about.

Another dreamer reported a frightening dream. She told us, "I'm in my bed when the shower turns on over my head. I try to turn away from it, but someone holds me down." Water being spiritual and cleansing, we all decided her time was here for a spiritual cleansing whether the ego thought she needed one or not. That's why she was being held down.

Another dream brought two surprising results. The dreamer told us, "I'm led into a room for a clemency hearing. A row of judges sat high above me. In the center was my boyfriend dressed in a suit and a tie. I left the hearing wondering what happened. Did I really get an added fifteen years?"

After talking this over from several different positions, it hit me, "If it were my dream," I said, "I'd be wondering what right he had to judge me!"

Her jolt told all I'd hit a sore spot. She said that hit home.

"He could also be you and you are being too harsh on yourself. Then again, if you've been fence sitting about your relationship with him, this would help make up your mind," I told her. She agreed and we left it that way. The second surprise came later that week when she learned he was dead. Perhaps this was a heavenly visit.

CHAPTER FOURTEEN

Thanksgiving has past and Christmas drew near. The prison chaplain had warned us the girls would be suffering deep mood swings. It always happened around holiday time. I found them to be more prone to tears, fears, thinking about missing home, and feeling everyone was against them. They needed this dream work now more than ever to keep some emotional balance. Some received warnings in their dreams about coming problems. One or two were able to avoid trouble but several were not.

Amazing things were still happening. One inmate dreamed of being with her youngest son (25 years old) in a cabin in the woods. In the dream they had a heart-to-heart talk about God. He listened to her and asked intelligent questions. Then they got in a car and went to visit grandmother in the nursing home.

The week after she reported this dream to us, she got an envelope with two letters in it. One was from her sister and one from her mother in the nursing home. It seems the boy had been missing for a year. He'd been in jail! A corrections officer had driven him home to the aunt's house. He walked in the door with a Bible in his hand, engraved with his own name on it. So, like the dream, he'd gotten religion. He went to visit grandmother in the home and stayed three and a half hours. He entertained all her friends and they just loved him.

First, she dreamed of being back together again and it happened with her family, then she had dreamed of talking about the Bible with him and he showed up with a Bible. How wonderful! There is a God! Good things do happen! She said she was speechless on reading the two letters. Luckily, a couple of other dream group members were in the compound with her and helped her explain the specialness of this to the others witnessing her meltdown. One of the other group members remarked on the mixed reaction this all got. One of two other inmates side stepped away, as if this were supernatural mo jo.

We who do dream work know this happens often. There are two possible explanations we cling to: 1) Someone greater than us cares about us and tries to help us. 2) Everything in life happens in our dream world first. We do have the opportunity to change an outcome, or at least our reaction to the outcome. In this case, she was sure God had given her advance warning this was going to happen. Now she hoped she soon will be visiting her mother and son also.

At a volunteer meeting where the upcoming holidays were discussed, the chaplain made a list of things we could provide for the women's gift bags. There were 300 inmates. As the chaplain named the brand and size of shampoo, and where to get the best price, a volunteer raised their hand and said their church would provide all 300. The chaplain was specific with brands, because all the women were to get exactly the same things. Down the list the chaplain read, and all items were pledged just like this. Little me, with no church or organization behind me, had nothing to give. I would help pack the bags. My husband and I provided three new irons for the compounds. The irons are used all day and wear out fast.

During the year, there's a list of items that can be donated and when I give speeches, I always ask in advance that these items be brought to the meeting. There is a store where the women can buy some items, but not all women have people who send then money. The chaplain keeps shampoo, denture adhesive, deodorant and a few other necessary personal items for them.

These women have asked to come to this prison. Some have sentences as long as twenty years. They have said they want to attend church and classes; they want to learn about a different way of living.

At the prison Christmas party, the volunteers stood alongside the sidewalk and as the inmates walked through, to reach the point where gifts were handed out, we all sang Christmas Carols. They also put on a play for us.

I feel a need to reflect, once more, on the statistics. One in every thirty-two people in the US are either in jail, on probation or paroled according to an article read in the Tampa Tribune. Think of all those on the outside trying hard to land in jail, the outstanding arrest warrants, the thieves not yet caught. Each year sixty thousand inmates are turned back into society. Will they have changed for the better or the worse?

The programs in this jail include GED, budgeting, parenting, anger management, addictions, and many introspection type classes. One volunteer records the women telling stories to send to their children. Worship services of several different kinds are offered and there are jobs around the compound such as landscaping, kitchen chores, cooking, law library, waste management, and more of which I'm not aware of. Don't be confused, the inmates are very much aware they are in prison. It's not nice!

I have enjoyed my work and hope to find another prison nearby, where I can try to be of help.

CHAPTER FIFTEEN

"In my dream," said the first dreamer on this night, "I watch a row of old-fashioned carriages traveling a rutted road in the country. We are old fashioned in dress, kind of like the Amish. The scene shifts and I'm out of the carriage and on horseback going across the ground, looking for a place to put my dynamite. Suddenly the ground erupts near me – like a small underground volcano causing a crater to open. Then I see another! I jump from one crater to another to avoid the eruptions. Although I wasn't aware of any family of mine in the dream, I suddenly felt that I must protect my son, who is a baby, and his grandparents."

Dreams often hold one inconsistency. This one was the age of her son who was actually 23. The chances were good that the son/baby was a part of her that she was protecting, a part not yet matured. This part was as vulnerable as a child, her inner child. She had been through enough. The dynamite would bring a huge change but maybe she didn't need it and was being warned about over-reacting to something soon. Looking back, soon after this meeting she did get demerits for bad behavior. One might say that her subconscious was emptying itself with several minor eruptions.

The covered wagons, the women decided, were a return to a simpler, more innocent time. On the move again, things were changing inside the dreamer, only this time with a horse. The women decided the horse was powerful – the dreamer's own power, or perhaps it spoke of a load she felt she carried on her shoulders, and she agreed that she had big guilt complexes over her children being put into their grandparents care.

She felt the dream was a warning and that she should return to a simpler way of viewing life in the prison.

One lady who was about to be set free after fifteen years seemed to be having dreams that were preparing her for life on the outside. At least she hoped this was true. She brought two dreams to this session.

"I see hundreds of small planes sitting in the ground. They are all pearly white, each with a splash of a different color. I'm thrilled. I once had a pilot's license. A man appeared and offered to teach me to fly these planes."

In the next dream I see a field of horses, brown with white spots. A veterinarian came to give them shots. I helped him give the shots and now he will let me ride them."

This seemed like a positive dream, one I wish I'd had. If it had been my dream, there were hundreds of ways for me to go. I was about to take off. I would finish the dreams the way I wanted, make my own wonderful ending.

If it had been my dream, I would take bows in front of this audience of planes (people) waiting to carry my words about dream work to hundreds of others. Imagine the speed both the horses and the planes could command.

We wondered what this lady's passion could be. I did notice the maintenance needed with both the planes and the horses and mentioned this caution to her. We may have a purpose in being born in this world, but we still have to work it, polish it, and live it!

The next dream was hard to contain. The girls wanted to take it at face value and did a lot of laughing at the red-faced dreamer's expense. My job was to keep them focused on the other possible meanings.

"I dream I have a crush on _____ (one of the guards). I'm on my knees as we kiss. At first the door is locked, then it's unlocked. I leave and go downstairs. Then I go with the same person and a baby into a loft. The scene shifts and I'm in a rocking boat in about three feet of water. It's rocking and making me nauseous."

One woman pointed out how in this person's dream of a week ago, she was rocking back and forth on a moving floor. Another shouted out that she's been nervous entertaining ideas like that also. This brought a big guffaw from the group.

I liked the locked then unlocked door and suggested she go back in the dream and get out of the boat, put her feet on solid ground. She needed to take charge where she could and be an authority figure. The kiss could be the coming together, something undecided was now made clear. The choice was hers. The authority figure represented the authority she had over herself. The group talked of the traps of such temptation. She agreed and promised to see the idea as metaphysical – meaning something else.

"I'm near a house in the woods," said the next dreamer, "It's night, dark and a flatbed trailer has a dead body on it, a man.

The smell of death is strong. The police will be coming. I hold a piece of his shirt, a dark flannel shirt, in my hands, wrapped in a newspaper. I need to find a place to hide it. I worry about my fingerprints being on it. The dream shifts. I'm a single mother whose baby needs milk. I'm in a hurry. I thought I had more but the refrigerator is empty. I must go to work. I only work four hours. I can be back with the milk then. I tell an older child to give the baby a bottle of water. I feel guilty and rushed."

"The dead guy," I told her, "is something that's dead for you – for so long it smells!" We almost got off track as the women tried to give advice on hiding a dead body – a little prison humor. Back on track, another person said she needed to let go of one small part, get rid of the part of her that was dead anyway. She suggested she not look back at that dead part anymore, no regrets, move ahead rather than try to bury it. The formula represented nourishment she needed (the baby, the milk, the dead guy, the shirt, all being part of her). She said not to accept substitutes. Another woman suggested she go to church services. She might find this long dead part of her there instead of buying it. It was not disappearing quickly and so may lead to something wonderful for her.

As we filed out the door that night, one inmate told me of a bunkmate's dream. Once it was out that these girls were taking my class, they became the dream 'experts' in their compound. Her bunkmate had a terrifying dream of a long hair being stuck in her throat. She kept trying to pull it out or cough it out, but she couldn't stop choking.

My student told her to consider it a health warning to get her throat checked, but also said she would get my opinion. In our short walk out the classroom door to lineup for transportation back to her compound and my entrance, we started to ask each other the magic questions. Describe yourself as the hair. What is your purpose? What don't you like about what you do? Her purpose, as we supposed she might answer, was to make someone beautiful. What didn't she like about being that hair? She was in the wrong place! We stopped there and laughed. She promised to take the questions to the dreamer and see what she came up with. It seemed a very fertile subject.

CHAPTER SIXTEEN

There was no report on the hair in the throat as our messenger got sick and didn't come to class the next week. More prison humor started this class as the ladies were congratulating one of the group for winning first prize in a pumpkin decorating contest. Curious, I asked if she'd carved it. Imagine the derision.

"Yeah, like they'd give us knives!" was the response of the women. I said, "I guess that proves I'm not the brightest gourd in the patch."

After the laughter died down a hand went up.

"I dreamed I'm sitting on the john when three or four guards come in looking for cigarettes. All I had was a lighter. It was a little stall and just so you know, smoking is a punishable offense."

I asked, "Do you smoke?"

"Yeah," she said, "but I'm trying to quit."

We talked about different ways of quitting and about those who've done it.

"I'm sure the guards coming in when you were in such a vulnerable position scared you," I remarked.

"Yeah, that and I would be in big trouble," she said, "I don't need another DR." (DR being a point system leading to punishment.}

If it were my dream," I said, "God would be helping me to give up smoking. I've had dreams that changed the way I ate. I had such a bad dream about cows I haven't touched beef in over twenty years!"

That astounded them. They couldn't imagine giving up beef. I did not share the dream as I knew they have no choice in their food.

One woman was behaving strangely. She hadn't attended this class more than a few times. She walked in, sprawled over two chairs, kept her head down, kept thumping her head and didn't take part, not even in the laughter. So, I turned to her next. She didn't want to share a dream she said, as hers were all too weird.

She felt her dreams were torturing her and that they were against her. Her dreams had predicted something, and it had come true. She would freak out when this happened, crying and carrying on. Once, she shoved the compound TV to the floor because of something she'd seen in a dream was showing on it.

No one understood her. "How can they (the dreams) do this to me?" she asked. She never said what happened on this day but told, instead, of another time when a new red-headed person was brought into her cell, and she recognized her from a dream. She was going off the deep end over these déjà vu incidents.

We assured her this was natural. People who recall their dreams often experience this. Sometimes we get to change events, but sometimes we don't. We don't need to get stressed when something difficult happens – we've been warned.

She then talked about all the negatives she would not forget in her life. The women talked to her about forgiving herself and moving on. After six years in jail and taking every class she could get, she felt she shouldn't have these negative thoughts constantly punishing her.

We spent a lot of time talking to her and I saw her write down the idea that to start changing things do a gratitude list each morning. I suggested she start with her pretty thick hair. That brought a smile to her face.

The women told her nothing good would happen for her until she got rid of her negativity.

She inquired about my book, its difference from other dream books and said she'd have a relative get her one. She was expressly looking for something she'd heard us talking about – that ah-ha feeling. We couldn't wait till she received one of her own. That would mean she was beginning to find her way.

One woman told this dream. "My ex wants money. I wear hiking boots and have $500.00 hid in each boot. He sees it. I'm found out!"

Many ideas were passed around, but the ah-ha came when one woman said, "If I was the money, the boots would be the prison I've been hiding in. I'm no use to anyone stuck in the boot. If it were my dream, I'd be about to get free."

This lady's dream the week before had her choosing between two doors. The one on the left had the number 6 on it. The door on the right had the number 7 on it. It didn't dawn on us until that night that the year was 2007. It was her year to open the door. It was what she had chosen, and it was the right one.

Another woman dreamed of holding a large, uniquely formed cat. "The head is of a large cat. The body is like a lynx. The front legs are of one animal and the back of another. The tail is curly and twisted. My cat wants to hide its tail, although it knows it is unique. I carry the large cat. Another inmate, with a stub for an arm, morphs out of a nearby dog and she has a perfect arm. I bend over, holding the cat and stay in that position until I get stiff."

I told her, "If it were my dream, and I'm the cat, I'd love this unique part of me." She proceeded to tell the story of her mother's reaction to her being gay. Her mother was afraid of how her friends would take the news. To nobody's surprise, they already knew it. This was her uniqueness. Don't hide your tail, meant you make others feel better about things they perceive as missing in themselves (ex. the arm).

Another woman had a breakthrough during the week. Her mother finally accepted a phone call from her, and they seemed to bond. They closed their phone conversation with both saying, "I love you." It always amazed us how our lives, those of us in this class, seemed to intertwine with each other's dreams.

CHAPTER SEVENTEEN

I had the privilege of watching a soul breakthrough, personal growth. It had been two weeks since we had heard from the lady who was freaking out. She showed up the week before with a haircut that was very becoming. She was quiet and asked a question or two. The next week she was much more vocal in a pleasant way. She was trying to understand my concepts, as she knew nothing else was helping her. She reported waking up scared. No dream was remembered, just a feeling of being scared. Since everything in the dream is a part of us, my thought was that her dreams, even though we had no idea what they were, could be that she was at war with herself. Our egos want to keep things as they are. Our true, often unconscious self wants to force some kind of change. Thus, the war.

I explained the analogy of us being hot-house plants. As hot house plants we are pruned throughout our lives. Pruned into a shape hoped for by our parents, teachers, and society that is not the true us. Our roots and branches are pruned. We're artificially fed until we reach the point we don't remember who we really are. Our inmate shouted out, "That's me!"

Before our session was over, she apologized to one of the women for blowing up at her during a math tutoring session. I felt this was real growth!

The next week I knew this growth/change would not happen easily. That week she said she was too upset to dream. She spoke of arguments with guards. I sat open mouthed, in disbelief. I told her they could make her life worse than it was. They could get her sentence made longer. She got upset again and said she was a human being and demanded to be treated as such. The rest of the group offered excellent advice as they had each been in her position. None of us seems to make any headway.

I switched gears slightly as I explained the power of attraction. What you think brings more of that action into your life. It seemed hopeless for her unless she changed her thinking. She said the prison psychiatrist had left and a new one had taken his place. She had taken this as a personal affront, told the new person he was no good and she wouldn't work with him. She acknowledged she needed help. The other women felt the same about the change, but they were more accepting and asked her to be patient.

One of the women suggested we pray for her, and I led them into meditation (a form or prayer). After asking our troubled lady where she would like to go, we took our minds to a beach in Hawaii. This was another of her hurts. She'd never been anywhere and had no idea what any beach or ocean or lake looked like. I led them to beach chairs at the water's edge that were like anchors. They would stay secure as the tide came in and covered them. They could breathe and see under the water, just like the fish. I suggested a special fish would come to them. They could ask any question and would receive an answer. After we came back to the room, the women shared their individual experiences. Our troubled lady was last.

Our inmate with the problem saw a fish in her meditation that was in a picture brought in by another person. The picture showed a man holding a largemouth bass by the mouth. The fish was almost as long as the man was tall. She asked it to take her anger far way. The fish agreed and she stuffed the anger in his mouth. The last she saw of the fish it was swimming away from her, belly bulging. She cried as she told us. I know this was a true breakthrough! The week after the meditation, she sat silently while a new inmate told the horrifying story of her life. Our angry lady whispered in my ear on her way out, "I'll be different from now on. I can do it."

CHAPTER EIGHTEEN

There were eight new women in my group this night. The chaplain had warned me about one. This inmate constantly disrupted the entire dorm each night by screaming in her sleep – several times a night. My introductory speech included my own need to defeat nightmares (demons) and how one other inmate, almost a year ago, followed my advice and rid herself of similar demons.

This woman insisted hers would never leave her. She relived, constantly, the shooting of her husband in front of her eyes and her own rape and beating that followed.

She insisted she was innocent and should not be in jail. I could only deal with where she was and what her dreams were telling her. So, we needed to break this recurring nightmare for many reasons.

I expressed the idea that some people believe everything happens for a reason. Jail time, like a long illness, could be a chance to heal more than the obvious hurt. It's often like a gift of time, time to get on a better path. The violence had taken place five years ago. She expressed a belief in God and so I quoted the Bible verse, "Fear not for the Lord is with you," and how my own dreams changed the verse for me to mean if you have fear, you don't have God. If you have God, you won't have fear. It took several reminders to myself, but eventually it became my insulation against harm. It's a tough statement to wrap oneself around, but it can do wonders for one's mental health.

She teared up when talking of how her bunkmates discussed her every day as though she was not there, about her screaming and keeping them awake. Some inmates were cruel and uncompassionate. I pointed out the sympathy she was getting from this group. I told her to find her confidants among this dream group. They agreed to be her sounding board whenever she needed to talk about her dreams. After talking almost an hour on her problems, we began demonstrating dream interpretation. Later that night, about two in the morning, it came to me that I should have given her something else to dream about. I'd tried, mentioning good times she must have had growing up. She negated that because she'd been abused and abandoned more than once. I tried to pull out her favorite movie or book. She could try to program her dreams rather than let the bad take over every night.

What came to me that night was that we all could have sent her prayers, or, better yet, a common story we all knew in our dreams. My mind skipped to Dorothy and the Wizard of Oz. I decided that in a future class I would talk of the parallels between her life and the story, such as the violent start of the movie, the search for something better – for a way home, looking for heart, mind and wisdom. Eventually the fraud of the wizard which proved that for which we searched was inside us all the time.

Looking for the yellow brick road made me chuckle, because I then realized a clue to this had been given me by the angry one. Her dream had been about a blond curl on her brother's head. The yellow brick road started in a tight curl and led to wisdom. I lay awake alternately praying for the angry one and the inmate with nightmares and seeing the new classmate (with nightmares) on that yellow brick road.

I hoped they would all return the following week so they could be part of this experiment, all of us sending the same dream to the new classmate. I was excited and hoped it would be her answer. She obviously suffered post-traumatic stress syndrome, but I felt enough time had gone by that, with our help, she would be able to put this behind her and find out why she was put on this earth. The next week, we talked a little about this. She mentioned feeling most fulfilled when she was nursing her first husband as he lay dying with cancer. She felt nursing in a hospice setting may be her calling.

She thought of her childhood and tried to remember what she fantasized; but could only talk of abandonment, beatings, abuse of all kinds.

I felt a need to talk with the chaplain about her. I was doing some volunteer work in the chaplain's office and asked her to help make sure this individual would return. Before the session was over, this dreamer was laughing and offering insights in others dreams. She became a real part of the group.

My plans for the Yellow brick road story done as a dream, did not happen. It seemed of all the people in the class, she was not familiar with the story of The Wizard of Oz. Must be a Mexican thing.

One dreamer reported her dream as being an inmate putting on a motorcycle helmet and being offered two rides on two different Harley Davidson motorcycles. We had some good natured laughs because I said, "If it were my dream it would be a nightmare." I gave a thumbs down sign for the Harleys. (My husband rides a Honda.) A couple of the new women were biker babes (as they called themselves), rode Harleys and for the rest of the class we bantered back and forth, laughing, joking about which was the better motorcycle. At the end I asked if they planned to come back. One said she enjoyed the class until she learned I preferred that other bike. She also gave me a big wink while she said it.

Another person shared, "I dreamed I was shopping with my grandmother and mother. This was something I'd truly loved to do before my grandmother died." I suggested she write them each a letter and tell them about the dream and thank them for the great shopping trip.

Another inmate who'd been with me a long time put her hand up. "I dreamed I was going on a magic carpet ride with a handsome American Indian man. The carpet had American Indian designs." She told us of a dream some twenty years before when she decided that the American Indian was her spiritual guide. She had a great time flying. I know from personal experience that a dream like this leaves you feeling fantastically energized for days. I envied that dream!

CHAPTER NINETEEN

The cycle of screams was broken! I'm not sure how much I had to do with it, but we broke the screamer's cycle of screaming. Right after our last class, she was reassigned to a different dorm. She loved the women there. She still talked in her sleep. The last night in the old dorm, she remembered being on a motorcycle in her sleep! She had never been on a motorcycle in her life and when she realized she was dreaming this, she woke laughing. The guards woke her up wanting to know what was so funny that she was laughing in her sleep. We did give her something new to dream about!

This class had thirteen women attending and it was an unruly group, as visitors from the first class also attended. Remember Joker? She had an old dream where she was saving friends from an old, wrinkled, toothless shark. This night, she reported dreaming she was walking along a beach and found shark's teeth! If it were my dream, I would be looking forward to getting some strength back. She drew a sample of the teeth on the board – it took up the whole space.

I mentioned they were unruly. The angry person got sidelined from being the center of attention as in the weeks before. I turned to her, and we tried to talk, but by this time everyone had turned to their neighbor and was having a private – so it seemed – conversation. A friend of mine said this was a good thing. They felt free and happy in this class. Well – Miss Angry and I could not get their attention back, so I pulled them into a meditation. On the way out Miss Angry whispered it was all right. She was working with the prison psychiatrist and taking steps forward.

CHAPTER TWENTY

I had spoken too soon. The screamer was not cured. She came in having just woken from a nap. She was uncommunicative, rubbing her eyes and appeared as though she was not with us even when I asked her a direct question. She said she was sleeping fine when I asked her. It wasn't until they were filing out at the end of the class that another woman from her dorm told me she still screamed in her sleep. Screamer stood right there and said she'd not been aware of this. It happened about 4:30 in the morning every day. Our screamer did confirm that another person had told her and threatened to put a sock in her mouth. Screamer is of Spanish decent, and I hoped, misunderstood this old American expression. I explained it to her and tried to reassure her no one would kill her that way. The guards were hurrying us along and anything further would have to wait until the next class. I hated that this gave the universe a whole week to let animosities build around her because of these dreams. The threat might have very well been real.

As I saw it, a village effort was needed to help her. If only the closest bunkmate would gently touch her or whisper that she was safe here, perhaps say she loved her and to go back to sleep. We can break this cycle.

It has been my experience that dreams which come in the morning are more about the future than the past. Dreams use what you know to tell you what you don't know. Her repeated dreams of her past trauma were using this as a symbol to tell her how to deal with her fears of her future.

During that evening, we again laughed about her dreaming of riding a motorcycle. It proved new things (good things) can be introduced into her psyche. She reported another dream. This was of going through a house and sprinkling holy water all over the house, on everything and every window and door. We all found this exciting for her. We felt she was being blessed. The house often symbolizes ones' life. Here it was being covered with holy water, a cleansing.

Another new woman raised her hand and told us, "I tried writing a question to God and put it under my pillow before I went to sleep. I got an answer!" She had our attention.

She felt she had alienated everyone she knew and loved by committing her crime and going to jail. Her question was whether her son would ever come back into her life. I asked his age, and he is 25.

"When I went to sleep," she said, "I dreamed of parasites, like sperm, digging backwards into my arms. There was blood and I poured hot water on them. They still dug in. When I woke, I knew the sperm represented my male child and he was backing into my arms – back in my life. I felt so happy! The blood was his blood connection with me."

I asked if at any time, especially the terrible teens, had she ever referred to him or thought of him as a parasite. They all laughed, and she said she probably had. We all marveled at God's sense of humor!

Another woman asked if we remembered her dream of throwing biscuits at a guard. The guard had been backing out a door to get away from the biscuits. She now knew the meaning of that dream. This guard had been transferred to another jail. Some say we live everything first in our dreams then in life. Somehow, the dreamer had tapped into this then future event.

Another hand went up and this dreamer said, "I dreamed I stepped out of my dorm, stood in the grass with my back to the fence. Over the fence came a barrage of golf balls. There is no golf course within the vicinity of the prison. It's a most unlikely, stubby field to be golfing in."

Other than an incoming message (the incoming golf balls) we were stymied as to any meaning for her and thought we'd have to wait for future dreams. During the week, after class, I e-mailed my other dream group about this dream and had two wonderful interpretations I couldn't wait to share with her. They both talked of being uplifted themselves upon reading the dream.

Ed, a member of my other weekly group, talked of stepping into the sun and turning his back (if it were his dream) on the fence. This would represent freedom for him. Looking back at the door represents opportunity, the opportunity to be free, even while in prison. "The golfer is the mind of the dreamer. Mind is creating illusory fences around the dreamer, creating only the illusion of confinement. The key is imagination and imagination will set you free," according to Ed.

Brenda answered, "The dreamer is now on the 'ball' and as unlikely as this field is for hitting golf balls, prison is an unlikely place for new ideas and sunshine, but they are there. She is the person hitting the golf balls, trying to get her own attention with all the thoughts that will get her to 'par'!"

CHAPTER TWENTY- ONE

There was good news! Our screamer now needed a new nickname. She had gone one whole week without a single nightmare! Dreams change when you finally pay attention to them and look for the message they are trying to send you. I think the message for her was to face the future without fear. What could she do to eliminate her personal worry? She needed to trust God was calling the plays of the game of her life. She needed to accept what she needed to, change what she could and have the wisdom to know the difference.

Putting her in a friendlier dorm sure made a big difference. I hoped she would continue to look forward, to remember her dreams, and to look for other messages. I have found in my other group work that people often come long enough to solve one problem and then quit. Problems don't quit! Dream mentoring, finding meaning in those messages of the night, can be very helpful in staying out of trouble!

This dreamer's only noise while sleeping reported during this week was giggling. During one episode, the guards stationed there shared with her that they also had to laugh when hearing her.

Our once angry lady led off this evening with a horrible dream which brought her upright in bed, looking for a man's head she'd just seen fly past her. "It was so real!" she kept saying.

"In my dream I'm riding along in my car, when another car goes flying into the air over me, tumbling end-over-end, twisting several times before it comes to rest on the ground. While the car was over me, I saw a head fly out the window of the car and bounce on the ground. I stop my car, get out and rush over to the vehicle, all the while looking for the head on the ground. A man gets out of the car. His head is on his shoulders! I'm puzzled! He is nasty. He says, 'What do you want?"

This dream seemed completely bad to her and had bothered the dreamer for several days. We discussed it until we decided the man was her and things were not as they appeared. It seems a warning that she might lose her head in a situation. But she didn't have to lose her head!

She said she had the dream Monday. She'd been fighting for the right to exchange letters with her son who was in another prison. She finally had written permission to correspond with her son, but still needed to educate the officer in the mail room to let her letter go through and let her see the last letter received from her son.

She went to the mail room and showed them her written permission. She told us that she behaved very meekly and received a favorable reaction from the mailroom staff. She'd finally won a round and now saw the meaning of this dream.

"What did she want?" the man in the dream had asked. It was not necessary to lose her head, figuratively speaking. She'd found one more reason to smile. Other good things were to materialize in the next few weeks. It was a pleasure to watch this lady's growth whether due to dreams or not.

Another inmate who after twenty years was hoping for her release to happen soon reported the next dream. All her dreams recently had been happy dreams. Again, "I'm happy. I'm having fun pushing Lee (another inmate) around the compound in a baby stroller. We're laughing, cutting up, and having a rowdy good time even though Lee has no legs."

Since everyone and everything in the dream can be a part of the dreamer, we turned to the baby stroller because it was odd. We decided that the wheels were the important part of the message and meant a speedy trip to the front gate. She liked this interpretation and we left it at this.

Another hand went up, "I'm driving my mother's car," she said, "My dead aunt is there but keeps changing into my aunt who is still alive. Back and forth they switch. My daughter is there also. We go to an old friend's house. I need an ace bandage for my sore shoulder. Instead of going straight up the porch steps, we go all the way around to the end of the porch. In an open door we can see four or five people sitting inside eating salad. Mom tells me to go inside. A man puts a 'Do Not Use' sign on the door and shuts it. We go back and get into the car. Where's my daughter? Mom says she's not wanted on this trip. I look and see her in my brother's arms.

After hearing her story, several elements of the dream became clear. She had a twelve-year-old daughter who had been in a lot of trouble. She had been taken by the state (big brother) to a group home. Going back to the beginning of the dream, the daughter was on the same ride as the rest of the family. The ace bandage represents the healing which needed to be done. The shoulder spoke of the weight this mother was carrying on her shoulders, the weight of guilt and helplessness.

The door to the family scene had been closed. The daughter was taking a different path. The inmate was happy about this turn of events. Her daughter might get the help she needed.

One thing that struck me was the number of family members that were also in jail. We asked this inmate about her brother, if he had custody of her daughter while she was in jail. She told us no, that they were co-defendants, and he was also in jail. We can only guess why the dream ended with the daughter in the brother's arms. Perhaps the situation might be that she was going into foster care, but that didn't mean she would be in a better situation. Not mentioning this, trying always to end on a positive note, we moved onto the next dream.

We ended this night with the usual hugs. It's best I don't know what they did to get put in such a place. I would not want my opinions to stand in the way of whatever help the dreams offered. We would take today and go forward from there, letting the dreams be our guide.

CHAPTER TWENTY-TWO

This new night brought us one more new person. She informed me right off that she was a pagan. "No God talk please." She'd been in this prison a week and had a lot of attitudes. "I follow my dreams all the time." she added.

When they all filed in, I acknowledged the new person and said we were of no particular religion. Whatever she wanted to be was okay with us if we could agree on one thing which was, we were all created by a higher being who still talks to us, guides us in our dreams. She agreed with that. I explained she would have to forgive me if I say God because that is my habit. She said that was okay.

In fact, different points of view make the interpretations interesting, I told them. Only the dreamer can recognize the truth of the dream and she might not think of what someone else has to say. It often happened to me with my dreams. I would take my dream to a friend, and they would say something I hadn't thought of.

The other women were eager to share the synchronicities that had happened to them, the things they saw in a dream and then experienced in their waking hours and kept thanking God for the messages that they were not alone. The new person didn't seem to mind.

Another woman, who'd been coming for three weeks, wanted to know how long she could stay in the class. We assured her she could come as long as she wanted. One lady had been with me more than a year. One would always need the guidance our dreams offered.

This triggered a memory of a dream in our new person. "I used to dream constantly of being in a car that is falling. All through my childhood I had the same dream."

"Perhaps it was telling you something about being out of control, needing to feel a sense of control about something in your life," I offered.

"It did come before I got into drugs at 13," she replied. "I was falling into a lot of trouble. My parents had good jobs. They just had no time for me. They never came to my school like other parents did."

"Weren't you able to join things, build a life of your own?" I asked.

"I was a cheerleader and popular."

"Those are fun things. Maybe you needed some more challenging things, things to wrap your mind around."

"Evidently," she replied.

"Well, just like contracting some disease that knocks you down, gives you time to contemplate life, you have time in here to ask those questions of yourself – who am I, why am I here on earth? What can I do to make the world a better place?" I said.

"That would be nice," she replied.

The once angry person was the subject of another inmate's dream. "I was out of prison and went to her house. She greeted me with a hug and said that I kept my promise. I followed through and she was happy to see me."

We put the words "house", "promise", "this other person," "hug," and "follow through" on the board and discussed them as if everyone and everything in the dream was the dreamer. What did we have? The dreamer, in the past had made a lot of promises about how she's starting a restaurant when she got out and was going to hire whoever was in front of her at the moment. We decided the big promise had a chance of coming true, but she should watch her promises. As it turned out, the person in the dream was related by marriage to the dreamer and they had met for the first time in this jail.

One of the inmates remarked about how the dream subject had calmed down since we first started doing her dreams. The dreamer, herself, had calmed down and had recently been engaged in decorating folders for all her friends. She did this by drawing beautiful flowers on her friends' folders. It seemed to have had a calming effect on her also. Changes were in the works and a good outcome was possible, according to the dream, for both the dreamer and the subject of the dream.

Our once angry woman dreamed of walking in a ditch in a tomato field. "I come to a pickup truck which takes me faster and then I see a two-story mobile home. Going inside I find there's no radio and no air conditioning. Going back outside and looking under the home, I find two loose wires. I try to push them up through a hole in the floor, but they keep falling out again. Suddenly some fingers appear from above and grab the wires from me. I go back inside to complete the connection so that I now have air conditioning and a radio."

"If it were my dream, that would be God reaching down to help me," said one inmate. Another remarked on the radio being communication. The dreamer reminded us her big wish had been granted – approval to mail and receive letters from her son who was also in prison.

I couldn't help but notice the beautiful ripe tomatoes. If it were my dream, they were there for the picking, and I was ignoring them. I wondered if there might not be better coming in her life; something she could pick in her travels. She said she'd spent many days in tomato fields, picking tomatoes. We left it at that but would come back to the dream another day.

CHAPTER TWENTY-THREE

I walked through the compound to our designated room and my once very angry friend met me along the way. She was the one with the dream of tomato fields and hands from above helping her make a wire connection.

We marveled over the hands from above helping make the connection, but we hadn't talked about the tomatoes. This had bothered me all week. Tomatoes are the fruit of life. She should have reached out and picked one.

This evening, once angry seemed somewhat dazed. She said a lot of stuff was going on – too much. She spoke of a new job in the prison culinary department for which she felt very special for getting but complained of no one taking over her cleaning job. She talked of how she couldn't live in filth.

Toward the end of the evening, I turned to her and told her my feeling of having missed something important in the dream by not pursuing the tomato field image. This is where I can get lost, as they say, not see the forest for the trees. The big truth was shouted out by the rest of the women. The tomato field had manifested! It was her new culinary arts position! Duh! Of course! Once angry went back into shock once more. She realized what the connection was that those hands from above had given her!

She gasped! "Nothing good has ever happened to me in my whole life," she said. "This is the first. I don't know how to act!"

"Just do the best you can," I told her, "Relax with the cleaning job. Give God a chance to push forward the right person. Praise that person for whatever she does. She'll improve."

Another woman – the one who'd written the note and put it under her pillow asking God if she'd ever get back into a relationship with her son, led someone else to do the same. She told a roommate about the experience. The roommate first denied that getting a message could happen, but she was so desperate to mend fences with her own daughter, she gave it a try.

That night she dreamed of sitting at a breakfast table with her daughter, laughing, talking and finally hugging. She was so amazed at how real it felt, at the depth of the feeling, how fulfilling and glad she felt for the confirmation. It could happen.

Other than that, it seemed a night to complain, and I let them vent for a while. The pagan person had put in motion a request to move back to her old prison. There was a large group of pagans, people who believed as she did and did not belittle her beliefs. She also missed things like a dog program and computer freedom. Not all agreed she was making a good move. Neither did I. The computer freedom scared me. They needed time for introspection! That's the weakness many on the outside face. Life is so full we don't have time to even acknowledge what we feel inside, nor do we take time to explore it.

She asked to stay in touch with me. We talked about her doing a dream group there. Since she was so new to dream interpretation there was a lot to teach her and perhaps a long-distance relationship would be beneficial to us both. Pagans take dreams as special, she said.

We quit early. I planned to write a handout detailing group dream work which any of them could use and/or give to their interested relatives on the outside. Hopefully the pagan would still be at the prison so I could give her the handout.

CHAPTER TWENTY- FOUR

On entering the prison this week, we, volunteer teachers and religious leaders, waited in a vestibule while a special head count was going on inside. Surprise counts and searches happen from time to time.

The subject of the pagan inmate came up in our conversation. I told of my first encounter with her and how I had high hopes for her. The pagan had agreed with me that someone a lot smarter than either of us talked to us in our dreams. One minister related her own conversation with the girl. She lectured the girl on disappointing her Catholic mother and the grief she was causing her mother by espousing such beliefs.

This girl was gone from the prison when we got to class. She had asked for a transfer to a different prison and got it. No wonder she wanted to leave. You can't change anyone's beliefs by hitting them over the head and telling them what they should believe.

You need to understand where they are in their beliefs and why. No change is as permanent as watching them gradually unfold their beliefs to include truth. It happens when truth is on your side. Chances also are that you might be wrong. Most of our belief systems are built on what other people have told us to believe.

Dreams teach truth. The message to change a way of thinking arises within you, unasked for. There is a big difference between knowing something because it comes to you in a dream or meditation and believing something because someone told you to.

I often wonder about the inmates who become new to Christ converts, how that helps them on the outside when their babies need diapers or food, a place to live, a job that pays enough.

Sorry I know that good is meant by these people and good happens. I hate to imagine a world without churches. But there is nothing like dream work to convince you that someone who loves you as you are, is with you always, helps you to build your sense of self-worth, shows you how to achieve better in a legal way. In other words, I wish church goers at least believed in dream work, and perhaps even taught it. What better way to reach masses of people who need to know how to hear God's voice?

Our first inmate to tell a dream had been a silent member of our group so far. Her dreams, it seemed to me, had finally decided she needed to take part.

"I'm standing there, and it starts to rain fish! That's all I remember – all I saw."

A couple of women went to the board and tried to draw the vision. We discussed fish metaphors as they did it, stinky, slimy, perhaps the plenty mentioned in the Bible, the change when Jesus fed the masses. We grabbed onto this last hoping she was beginning to open to her subconscious. It occurred to me, later, that she could simply be a fish out of water. Time would tell.

The evening had more than one fish. The next dream teller was an inmate waiting to go home. She was in for committing a DUI fatality, the victim being her own son who was in the car with her.

She told this dream, "I'm standing at a lunch counter. I have a long list of what I want. That and more is piled up on the counter in front of me. They also put a live fish on the stainless-steel counter. It keeps looking at me. I say they've given me too much and how would I cook the fish anyway? A person behind me says, 'with your lighter.'"

There was much symbolism! Talk about a fish out of water! Thinking of the lighter, I asked if she smoked and she said, "of course, we all do here."

If it was my dream, I would take it as a health warning to lose weight, stop smoking. Instead of a stainless-steel counter, I see a morgue slab. If I were the fish, I'm still alive. I'm waiting to see what will happen to me. If it were my dream, I have all I asked for and more. Time to go home. With my lighter the dream is saying to lighten up (physically and mentally). I think the message would be to take me, the fish, and put it back into the water where it belongs, back home with her family.

Another inmate told her dream, "I'm driving with my boyfriend when we see a large snake on a wall. It has black and white spots like a cow. We stop, bag it, and put it in the trunk of the car. I'm afraid it will get free and come through the backseat. My boyfriend says not to worry but he stops the car again and gets out to open the trunk, and open the bag, and show me that the snake is safe inside.

The snake's head comes out of the bag. Out of its mouth comes a baby snake with two heads."

Ever heard the expression about the snake being let out of the bag? This person had just written a nasty letter to her boyfriend, but, thankfully, she tore it up, she said, without mailing it. The next day she received a large packet of letters, from him, that had been held up in the mail room. All letters going in and out get read, therefore the hold-up of mail. Often, a bunch of letters from the same person get delivered together to the inmate.

Perhaps the dream had been her fears about sharing the car, representing her life, with him. Worse still, in the symbolic world, she was letting him drive her life. The snake has (among other things) a sexual connotation, as was stuffing it in her trunk. The three heads could be about the number of children he'd fathered. The one positive was the cow spots on the snake. The spots reminded us of amoeba that have a changeable form. Her feelings about him did change when she got the mail.

Another woman also dreamed of the man in her life. "I walked into my bedroom and my husband was in bed with another woman. I turned around, opened a door across the hall and lots of light came out of this doorway."

"This could be literal," I told her, "maybe he is doing this, and maybe you fear he's doing this, maybe it's replaying a scene from the past. Maybe it's not him. Everything and every person in the dream can be a part of yourself. Look to some part of your life where you feel you are being screwed (if you are the woman in the bed). How are you not being true to yourself? Perhaps it is a fear of being found out. Letting go, taking the other door is enlightening. Perhaps you should be looking in a new direction, opening other doors in your mind. Find other talents, opportunities."

She said her mother did not like this guy and wanted her to leave him. We all agreed she should listen to her mother.

CHAPTER TWENTY- FIVE

Remember the inmate who dreamed of the raining fish last week? I had hoped it signaled a breakthrough for her. Her dream this week seemed to be pointing in that direction.

"I'm standing in the shower at home and see a man, away off through the window, the other side of the yard. He's watching me with binoculars. I'm scared! I can't hide. He sees every step I take. I hear a knock on the door. It's him. My mother interferes by getting to the door ahead of me. The man backs up a step and says only I can touch him."

If all the people in the dream are a part of the dreamer, if it were my dream, the man who saw everything would be my subconscious self, watching me. It was good that I was finally becoming aware of him.

In Jungian psychology, our opposite side or subconscious self, in a women's case the man\animus (Jung's term) represents our highest good. He's the character that brings all the other characters into the dream to tell us something we badly need to know. I call this a message from God. The character often, but not always, is someone we know, sometimes good, sometimes bad, depending on what we need to know to make our life better.

It was good she was becoming aware of her subconscious self. In this dream being in the shower could be symbolic of needing to come clean about something, or an actual cleansing taking place, in her heart and mind, of her ideas and ideals. It was interesting that the mother interfered (in her words). Perhaps all her mother's advice had not been good. Even if her advice had been good, we need to discover and nurture (mother) our uniqueness in order to lead a good life, hence the mother figure as a symbol.

She was extremely grateful for the interpretation and the dream. First, she'd been afraid and now she wasn't. She was hopeful for the first time in a long time.

It is a privilege to watch a permanent change come over a person who needed it as badly as she did.

The next dream included fish again! Our inmate dreamed of fishing with her brother, "The water is dark and murky. He catches a catfish on a big hook. The fish is yelling 'ow-ow-ow'. I say I will help, hold on, I will get the needle nosed pliers."

We agreed she was the fish, caught on a big hook. Maybe the brother was a metaphor for the State of Florida. Big brother = big government? If not, perhaps he was the part of her that got her in trouble with the law. There was hope in the fact that she could fix it. She could relieve her pain. She knew which tool to use and where to find it.

When beginning to work with someone new, the dreams often seem to be telling me where this person's biggest concern in life is, or should be, and we go from there. She got caught and it is saying ow-ow-ow. It's up to her, how she behaves from now on, in prison and out, if she gets caught on that hook ever again. If we haven't rightly guessed the meaning of a dream, other dreams with the same theme will continue until the dreamer does 'get it'.

CHAPTER TWENTY-SIX

I returned to prison after a five week vacation. I gave a talk at an International Association for the Study of Dreams (IASD) conference in Sonoma, California, encouraging other dream workers to volunteer for this work in their prisons. Then my husband and I met for a visit with our children and grandchildren in upstate New York.

I had a lot to share with the women in prison that I'd learned from the other conference speakers and wondered if they would all still be there. But first, I have a most amazing story to share about my trip.

A funny thing happened on my way to the San Francisco\Sonoma area. On the long leg of the journey, between Atlanta and San Francisco, my seat mates were a nice man and his nine- or ten-year-old son. Since they were engaged in lively conversation, we didn't exchange words until we were about to land. When this man found out where I was going and what I was doing, he asked for a thousand word article for his publication, Sarasota Downtown and Beyond. That's a wonderful gift from the universe to me to begin with but I wasn't done with them.

I picked up a bad flu-like condition while at the conference and had to reschedule my return flight a day early and guess who sat next to me this time? The same two guys! In my ill state I felt I was with family. Steve Rabow, publisher of

<u>Sarasota Downtown and Beyond</u> printed my article on page four of his next issue and added a sidebar about how we met and the coincidence of our return journey as well. I don't think either of us really believed it was a mere coincidence. Everything happens for a reason. Time will tell.

My first night back at prison brought me several new, eager, faces and a couple of old regulars as well. The first night everyone had dreams to decipher and questions about where dreams come from. I guess it pays to take a break occasionally. When I first speak to a woman, her dream seems to be pointing out where she is in her life right now. The dream tells us both what she needs to work on to begin her healing process.

The first inmate to report a dream told this, "I'm at home with Mon and Dad when Mom gets a phone call saying she's won the lottery. They need to drive to Chicago to collect their winnings. After pleading to go along they finally let me. We climb up in the semi-truck with Mom driving. After a while, she gets tired, and I take over. I see the tips of my sneakers touching the pedals. The road has been straight but now it becomes winding, and I lose control. We all feared for our lives. I shouted; we're going to die! But I was able to halt the truck in time."

Our first timers even caught the words about losing control and the twisted road when she took over. She would have been better off to obey her mother! She's coming to grips with wanting control of her life and feeling guilty for what she did to her family.

Another woman with mother problems had this dream, "I, and a bunch of people behind me, are watching my mother through a window. She's eating a donut with pink icing. Will she find the $10,000.00 token hidden inside? She stops eating and pulls the last of the donut on top of a brick wall."

When we asked what her relationship to her mother was, she said she'd probably go and live with her when she got out. Her mother, however, was a very negative person and our dreamer wasn't sure she could live with that.

"If I was the donut," I asked her to think about this for herself, "would the token be what is left of my true value? If I go live with her, will she consume me completely with her negativity?"

Someone else pointed out that donuts are sweet, and pink is love. Perhaps we are not seeing Mom's true intentions. One thing for sure, God was suggesting she solve her problems with her mother, first, before anything else can happen.

One inmate's dream showed hopelessness. "I'm swimming with a guy when a squid and an octopus attack him. He swims to a dock, puts his arms on the dock to steady himself and says, 'I guess I'm going to die young.'"

'If it were my dream," I tell them, "I would look to somewhere in my life where some person or set of circumstances are dragging me down. (Jail would do it.) I'm thinking of the suction cups the two sea creatures have. Suction cups could suck me under." Although this might be how she felt, maybe even entertaining a wish to die young, there was hope. He saved himself on the dock. He is the animus of Jungian psychology, her male opposite, who had come to awaken her of something. She needed to care about herself, work to save herself.

Another inmate showed her doubts as to her ability to get along in the 'real' world. "In my dream, I have taken my daughter inside our apartment for a little rest. A man knocks on the door and makes an obscene gesture. I get very angry, go outside and blame the people in the street for sending him. I've had enough of that kind of living and proceed to make obscene gestures of my own. I ask myself, 'Will I ever know how to act in society?" The end of the dream, the last thought, says it all. The rest points out a need to protect myself from outside influences.

Another dreamer said she was trying to get rid of a dead body in a box. "I tried to get all the body into a box, but the hinges of the box are on the verge of breaking. I fold the body's legs up; they snap and the bones break. I need to find a different place to put the box. Its odor would make it too easy to find here. Then I remember my prints are on the box. I am so afraid I'll be found out."

It took a while to dig into this, they were all trying to give her advice on getting rid of a dead body. Believe it or not, more laughs. In the dream I saw a search going on. If I were the box, what are people trying to stuff into me? I must ask myself, am I buying what the various classes here in prison are trying to teach me? The dead person was who I used to be. Many changes are coming. Can I hide who I used to be yet keep that part of me? The snapped legs could be the end of the old foundation or way of thinking about life. This is good because that way landed her in jail! This could be another very interesting group and I hoped we would stick together long enough to see some real change, as I had with other groups.

One woman, however, seemed proud and still attached to her drug habit. Almost everything anyone said reminded her of some experience with drugs, to the point the eyebrows of the others went toward the ceiling.

I've learned a lot about human behavior from them. I've learned a lot about them. Most were abused at an early age. A couple of them have had children die when they were young. A lot have other family members also in jail.

We are deciphering a lot of dreams, but there are times I feel we get away from the basic system psychologist Carl Jung laid out in his studies. On some nights they enjoy short movies I've brought. These we interpret using Jungian methods. There is more on this in part 2 of this book, we have good discussions after, as if it were our dream. This will be beneficial when they no longer have the benefit of a group like ours.

However, I'm getting discouraged and don't know why. I feel it is tied to the lady whose prime interest seems to be the good times she's had with drugs. I wonder if I'm capable of handling this. It's time for some miracles, Lord.

CHAPTER TWENTY-SEVEN

I'd been depressed for a few weeks and have finally figured out the cause. It is the person who talks quite freely about doing drugs and turns most conversations into stories of the good old days when she was using them. I finally realize that she has no intention of bettering her life. Part of me agrees with her. She has been doing drugs since the nineteen-sixties, thirty-five years, she says. Is it possible to change? When I asked how she is doing without them in prison, one of the other women said this is considered a vacation from drugs. Most plan to go back to them. So, a new light bulb in my head has finally lit. The light is encouraging me to question why is she taking this class?

After thinking this over I planned to approach this as one more challenge that God would get me through, teach me something more, like the lessons I learned with the two people who screamed all night and the very angry woman. I hoped the other four in this class had not been held back because of her attitude. I planned to put in more home time this week on their dreams, sort them individually from the beginning and see if I can find more meaning than we have already. I wondered if this long-time drug user ever thought about what else she could do with her life if she'd not got caught up with the drugs. We would get an answer to that before we were done with her.

Her dream this class went like this; "I'm back in the woods. We've done a lot of camping over the years but this is a place I've only seen in my dreams – several dreams. There is a cabin and four trails. One trail leads to the lake, one leads to a river, one leads to a waterfall and one to a beach where the water is a beautiful light green, like you see when you go to the southernmost tip of Florida. I have a few buds of pot that I smoke in a pipe. I'm expecting people to come. I hope I have enough buds of pot to share and then I can show them my favorite place by the ocean."

This was when she made clear to me that she expected nothing in her life would change, since she'd been doing it for so long. However, I saw she feared running out of pot. Next week I would get into this aspect of the dream with her. What will she do when she runs out? According to the conversation surrounding the dream, the others suggested she was selling it. She admitted she shared with her friends.

Another inmate had a very fanciful dream. "I'm watching flying candy. I'm so starved for chocolate! I saw red wrapped Crunch Bars, yellow Mr. Good Bars and more. I'm standing with a bunch of people watching them fly by." Of course, they probably felt the good things in life are passing them by. If it's the colors that are important, red may be passion, yellow joy; we forgot to look at the color charts. Did I say I was distracted? Another detail to cover next week.

Another inmate reported a dream where she was standing in front of a townhouse that seemed familiar. "I hear the phone ringing, first a loud ring, then a soft one, like an echo. I open the screen door and go in. Before me is a set of very narrow stairs leading up. Everything is beige and white. My ex says, 'Don't come in my room!' I get angry and take off my blue shoe and whip it at the door and miss. I take off a second shoe and do the same. I take off a third shoe, throw, and finally hit the door. The thought goes through my mind – three shoes? I notice there were two bedrooms. If the other bedroom is mine, where will my daughter sleep?"

We heard echoes with the two rings of the phone, echoes of the past perhaps. Going up is usually a good thing. You can see things from a higher perspective. The narrow passage can sometimes indicate the birth canal, birth of a new way of living perhaps. But the door is closed. Blue can be wisdom, peace. Perhaps the way to wisdom and peace is to get that door open. The house is not big enough for all of them. If the house is symbolic of her life, it needs to grow. I'd say she is growing, what with three feet, her foundation is growing. I suggested she take all the classes she could get, watch constantly where she has a big interest, or something seems easy, or a talent. She can possibly make a living for herself from what she learns in one of these classes. In all, taking the premise that the ex, locked in a room was part of her that had been locked up tight not letting new ideas in, this seems a good dream, a growing dream. She needed to write three personality traits for the ex. See where they or similar traits were also in her personality for a clue to what she needs to set free.

She was happy with this interpretation as she had recently signed up for a class in math, a subject she feels capable of doing.

CHAPTER TWENTY-EIGHT

Now, back to the woman, my latest challenge, who had the wall of 35 years of pot smoking built around her. We really got into it this week. During this week, I spent some time in meditation with her dream, about being in the woods with four trails leading to water. It came to me that she was afraid to go into the woods. The woods meant getting off the path she was most familiar with, perhaps bumping into obstacles (trees) and issues she couldn't handle. Either way, all trails led to water and the spiritual side of life. The small lake, which was not her favorite place, indicated her small life. The river was a place where she could go with the flow of things, but she did not know where it would lead. The falls held either a kind of danger or a cleansing. Either way, if she entered the falls, she'd not be the same person when she came out. The ocean was the ocean of life, the big picture. She wanted to show this to her friend.

The way I deal with my own dreams is to become the various things in the dream. I did this with her dream. I became the pot. I'm being stuffed into the pipe. Where in her life did she feel she was being confined, stuffed down? Was there enough of her to last, to share with anyone else? How much time does she have left? She may feel herself breaking up into small pieces.

In class, I asked if any of these thoughts rang true with her. She then admitted she did not want to be a drug person. She feared coming back to jail. And everything I'd said was very true. She feared trying to support herself when she got out, so logic took her back to the old ways, the old friends; but she didn't want it that way.

Finally, I had a chance to help her. A chance to get her true feelings out into the open where she could see them, and work on solving some of these problems, give her some backbone. There had to be a way and the dreams would help. Her dream this week took her back to the art store where she used to work. She wanted a book to read. A fellow inmate had taken all the books. She saw one left, but it belonged to the boss. She promised to bring it back if the boss would let her read it.

"At lease there is no pot in this dream!" she quipped. They all cheered. We saw a lack of security also, her big fear, that she was too late to get what she needed most. Perhaps being educated was being symbolized by a book. I would take this into meditation at home and see if I could have any more insights.

I asked her to direct her dreams this week. "Before going to sleep, write down these questions and hold them in your hand and your mind. God, why was I born? What was I supposed to do with my life? How can I support myself?" This was a homework assignment for her. Other inmates tried the exercise as well. We often learn from each other's dreams.

The next dream reported that class helped all of them.

The next inmate said, "I dreamed about rolling pot into cigarettes. I couldn't get it to stay in the paper. I tried several times and got really frustrated when the pot kept falling apart."

"You're done with your addiction!" I said. "You don't need to do this anymore."

"Thank god!" she replied. A big smile came on her face, and I recounted to them some of the other dreams the inmates had reported when their addition lost its hold on them. They all know now that it can happen.

CHAPTER TWENTY-NINE

The woman who had been using drugs for thirty-five years had spectacular success. It seemed God had been waiting a long time to get her attention. There were five dreams and six visions, sentences, or scenes she reported in this one week. As she read them in class, she said every word applied to her. First came the words that she could find a job in a half-way house or a home for battered women. She said that seemed like a possibility. Then she dreamed that she was being congratulated for making a quick change, six weeks. This I thought was telling what might be coming. Her immediate thought was about the time the court gave her probation for using drugs. She gave up smoking it on that day. That was probably what the congratulations were about, reminding her that she could do it. Her downfall was a court ordered surprise visit to her home where they found her stockpile for her 'friends'.

The next dream was about getting frustrated in a hospital. She saw two things; one was her own battle with cancer and the other was her intolerance of inept people. Then her left arm ached. She could have been laying on it, but she said her left arm has no lymph nodes and she is super careful of it.

She saw a bottle of cold water with ice cubes in it. In my estimation, and I still think this is true, it was a symbol of bottled-up tears. Her interpretation was that she was a cold-hearted person.

Words came about there being something she wanted to achieve but never thought she could. Her related memory was of an intelligence test her brother once took. Her brother has two degrees now and had the highest score on the IQ test in the history of that college. As a favor, they also tested her. She scored higher.

One dream had her watching a boy roll down a hill and hitting his head. She laughed and wondered if he would do it again. God is waiting to see if she will roll downhill again.

She saw a backyard being planned. She owns property and just knows that no one is taking care of her yard.

The last image was about an invention. She said she once had a great idea for an invention. She said that being a druggie, she just talked about it a lot, and didn't do anything to follow through. Two years later, someone gave her a present of the same thing she had envisioned. This was a 'could have been'.

I consider this a breakthrough. She was looking at possibilities for the future. Her mind was open to the stories of her dreams, and she admitted she did not want to come back to prison. She also acknowledged that she knew she'd have to move far away from anyone she knew in order to lead a different life.

The bible tells of three ways to contact God. One is through the casting of lots. One is through your own dreams and the third is by asking a prophet to dream for you. Since the world seems short on prophets, and who knows how to cast lots, we'd best learn to capture and understand our dreams.

The Old Testament holds several turning-point-dreams. These are dreams that changed a person's path, set a course for a better life, much like what we have been talking about. Jacob, in Genesis, was being secretly groomed by his mother to take over the family inheritance from his brother Esau because she had received a message from God while Jacob was still in the womb. Jacob's reason for going along with the deception of his brother and his father, Isaac, was purely greed. He was on the right (destined) path for the wrong reasons. His promise could not happen until he woke up to his true potential. He was lost in the wilderness for years. He could have been eaten by wild animals, he could have been killed by bandits, he could simply never find his way. Many people have these wilderness experiences and never leave home.

One of the most famous stories of the Old Testament is of Jacob's dream of heaven opening and a ladder coming down to earth on which angels traveled down and up, down and up. This was his turning-point dream. Now, you and I have all witnessed turning-point dreams from these prison women. Rehabilitation is possible through dreams. We are born with this ability. Let us use it for the good of all.

I hope I have inspired you to record and follow your own dreams and, if you get a chance, lead a group somewhere – maybe even in prison. Following is some information on doing this. There is my philosophy as it has been building. Also are some handouts that will help you personally, and to use in a group if you choose.

Good luck and God bless. Carol

PART TWO

Dream Work

Philosophy and Mechanics

CHAPTER THIRTY

If working dreams can bring so much change to the lives of men and women in prison, what can it do for those of us not in prison? It has been said that we often make our own prisons with our own belief systems, who we think we are, who we think our parents and teachers said we are, what we feel we must do to get along in society, mistakes we've made in the past, our guilty feelings.

Then there is also our way of thinking. To quote the book <u>Meditations from Conversations With God</u> by Neale Donald Walsh, "You do not live each day to discover what it holds for you, but to create it. You are creating your reality every minute, probably without knowing it."

How many of us get up in the morning wondering what this day will bring? I know I do it more often than I'd like to admit. And with good reason, the best things that have happened to me I've not asked for. They come spontaneously. Or did they? Did I miss recording the promise of this happening in a dream? Did it come as a result of an action I took previously? Is it a reward or result of something else I did? I like to think that. It's happened so often that I've come to believe it.

When first working with my dreams, I made lots of changes in my life, what I ate, what I thought about myself, how other people affected me. I picked up new talents and worked on them. My first writing job came in my mailbox. How spontaneous is that? I shall always feel that was a reward. There have been several others and they are recorded in my book, <u>When God Stood Up:</u> The dreams led me to a much better life!

Personal dream work has been good to me, but when doing dream work in a group you learn from each other, and you help more people and you see more positive change at a much faster pace. It reinforces your beliefs about dreams.

I'd like to see more people become conversant in dream group work and take it into a prison. If you are taking the challenge and walking into that prison room for the first time, it's a good idea to try to come to common ground with the inmates as far as beliefs. You don't have to buy into my beliefs that have evolved from my own dreams and experience. Yours will do just as well if you leave the final authority to the dreams. None of us can positively know everything. Remember the old Indian saying about not judging until you walk a mile in that person's shoes.

The first night, you need to give them good reason to stick with you and with dream work. You might mention healings that have come about because of dream work. Give them some hope for internal change. Perhaps you have a story of your own that resulted in your continued interest in dreams. Talk about the truths that come out of the dreams that can change their lives. Tell them about that unknown someone, who originates the dreams, who is smarter and greater than themselves, who loves them and wants to make life better for them.

The rest of the time that first night you'll be instructing them as to group work. A good handout this first class is a list of dreams from the Bible. They often need this to counteract any negative thoughts others might try to impose on them about working dreams. I have a partial list for you in the appendix. Please copy it! They can look up the stories on their own time,

Talk about mental prisons! I have a theory on how we've each built our own mental prisons and how we need to undo the harm these thoughts have caused in our lives. By undoing that harm, we benefit not only ourselves but society as a whole. Each of us, as an individual, helps build the pyramid of society. The world tensions are a mirror held up to our personal tensions and magnified.

As we see more clearly our role and ease our own tensions, our changing spirit helps to build community and world peace. It's worth a try. It is something we can do! Christians talk of the second coming of Jesus. I say He's been here a long time. He's working with us in our dreams and meditations. After finding the Aha of a dream, good happens in our lives and the Bible says that all good comes from God.

Coming to 'know' your creator makes a big difference in your life as the stories of the women in prison have shown thus far. They have no doubt who is working with them in their inner life. Introspection is a lost art; it takes time, but it is time well spent.

On the outside, I started a meditation group that meets before church each Sunday. On the very first day a man asked for interpretation of a dream he'd had that week that he could not push from his consciousness. Some dreams are like that. He dreamed of driving on a dirt road alongside a river where the water had risen to the top of the riverbanks. It was running fast, rolling wild, and full of life. On the other side of him, in a distance, he saw a regular road with a few cars traveling along it.

As we live in Florida and approaching hurricane season, he worried that it was a prediction and perhaps he should move away for the summer. I tried to shed some light on the dream before meditation, but I had no ideas other than what he'd already guessed.

Our meditation consists of soft music playing, a suggestion that takes us, mentally, to a private place where we sit in the light of healing, and we can get answers to any questions. There I leave them in silence with their own minds for fifteen to twenty minutes before I bring them back. We do this in prison, as well, as it stimulates our dreaming process. Then they share their experience, if they want to.

Unplanned, his dream became clear to me. This man has led a group of people studying their spiritual sides for years. The dream has him riding the ridge between those people open to their spiritual sides (the natural river of life) and those on the other road, not interested, not aware or just too busy. The dream was showing him that the number of people finding this connection with their creator was rising significantly, filling the riverbed. The number of people finding their spiritual self is growing rapidly. The other road was not as busy as it once was.

This is a good message for us all, a hopeful heritage for our children and their children.

Some people believe the disasters we experience on a large scale are trying to also bring us to this 'knowing' of our creator. We (as a country and individually) make changes when a storm wipes out a city, or an earthquake happens, or terrorists hit. Our changes don't last very long. This country with all its generous people, does not get the message. We do not understand the difference this sacred communication makes. Now is the time to learn how to do this. The important changes are the changes we make within ourselves. This is made easy by catching our dreams.

When dealing with prison inmates we don't need to know what happened to them in the past, what they did to get there. Little by little the stories will come out but, frankly, I do have preconceived ideas about prisoners always professing innocence and take every story as a grain of the truth. They will want to present their best to you, kind of like the stories about us that we tell ourselves. Dreams will address where we are today, right now, and our inner, higher selves look to inform us as to the best future for us. The dreams will lead us to make better decisions, think more highly of ourselves, and live a better life, whether we will be behind bars for the rest of our life or not.

Prison inmates are people who've made grave mistakes. Who hasn't?

I find that if I know as much as possible about a person, as sometimes happens with my outside dream group, I can make better interpretations. But nothing is more powerful for them, leads to a more permanent change, than when the person discovers the truth for him/herself.

Change is necessary if you've gotten yourself behind bars but what if you're not in prison or what if you view your life as good? We can also be off track and many of us are. Where and how do we get off track? One analogy I like to use when giving lectures is that of a hot house plant that's been pruned to be what it is. The Bonsai tree hobby pops to mind but what I see is more of a plant that's been similarly pruned to where we see ourselves as the only big leaf on the plant. Over the years we've been pruned, by well-meaning people (we've done it to our own children). We've tried to help them become good society members, earn a good living, help others be happy.

Now, as that pruned leaf, we are unaware that our roots have also been pruned. However, if we take a closer look, through introspection, meditation and dreams we see the spirit of these parts are still there. In spirit there are deeper roots, a stalk or two attached to us and more leaves that represent our now subconscious inner self. If we recognize these perhaps, we can also claim that flower that waits to crown our beauty, help us love ourselves and only then, truly, love others.

One of the dream symbols that most often came to us, giving us clues of us being more than we think we are, is that of exploring rooms of a house. As we open each new door, we find a room with amazing gifts and opportunities or empty rooms we can fill any way we want, or the room is full of junk that needs to be cleaned out (simplify your life).

Many before me have likened life to an iceberg floating on the ocean of life. Our conscious minds are aware only of what floats above the water. This is the part where we influence each other and have been influenced. There is much more of ourselves below the surface. Hiding there in our subconscious mind is everything we've ever known or experienced and our connection with that someone greater than us. This is where our dreams come from. That spirit inside us, our higher self, remembers what we came into this world to do. It remembers and tries to remind us to use our talents. It causes trouble in our outer world when we neglect them.

It has been proven in laboratory testing that we can better live without food than live without dreams. Dreams are an integral part of our being even if we don't remember them. They attempt to help us solve all kinds of problems even before they come up. It is our conscious minds, the pruning we've been through, the conditioning, the ideas we hold based on what we've been told or experienced that keep us from following our 'gut' instincts. It is much better for us to keep an open mind when we can look at the messages from inside.

The place in the Bible where Jesus asks the little children to be brought to Him translates for me to mean that it is better for us to come to God with the minds of children, with a willingness to learn, with the mindset that we can still learn something. This would apply also to the meek, the going through the eye of the needle not as a puffed-up, know-it-all.

So, when dealing with prison groups and any group where there might be more than one theology represented (and non-believers too), set theology aside. Dream study has nothing to do with theology and everything to do with developing our spiritual side. The truth that comes from your dreams may surprise you. Truth can be different for different people. Finding and trusting your inner voice is big enough!

My hope is that the first night you will find a way to share these thoughts with the group.

CHAPTER THIRTY-ONE

I'd like you to understand the mechanics of both group dream work and your own personal dream work. In the group work I use what some consider an older model of finding the meaning. It works for me.

Write the key words of a dream on a black board or pad of paper on an easel. This helps hold the focus of the group. Several will have a story to relate or a feeling about the first word. As one person tells her related key word story, we can easily slip back to the board when she's done, and we've all discussed our own similar experience. Another reason for a place to write is that some dreams just cry out to have a drawing and the dreamer, or another with an idea, can come up and clarify something by making that drawing.

Sometimes the dream is very self-evident. However, one dream can contain messages on more than one level. As Rev. Jeremy Taylor likes to say, "A dream uses what you know to tell you what you don't know." Therefore, we always to try dig a little deeper.

It is true that in times of stress, our dreams become more active. These inmates are such wounded souls that we never have to dig very far for direction for them. I think this is the reason we can cover so many dreams in a short time. And this is the reason such major changes can be made in the way they view themselves.

Everything, every person in the dream can be a part of the dreamer. By writing clues of an object's personality and relate it to the dreamer's personality and/or how this might be used in the dreamer's life, we often receive our first Aha. If the object is a fish, we write in the borders about God feeding the multitudes or abundance. We also find adjectives like slimy, smelly, nourishing, and something big on the line. It is surprising how many metaphors a group can come up with. What is the name of that variety of fish? Is there a play on words here?

If you are working alone, write your dream on the middle of a piece of paper leaving large margins where you will fill in these metaphors and adjectives. It is helpful if you have one other person you can tell the dream to whether they understand dream work. They may see something you should have seen but didn't.

Sometimes the dreams are what I call a marking of God's time and you'll find no meaning. In a few days you'll see the exact thing happen. It's always good to keep dreams written in a journal so that you can go back and check.

If there is a strange object, and usually there is, put yourself in the place of that object. A lady in my outside group dreamed of looking at wallpaper in a bedroom that had repeat prints of frogs. One of the frogs fell down and she picked it up and put it back on the wall. She thought the pattern was neat. My own thoughts were that she was about to leave this pattern of her life become a real frog rather than a reprint of several others. Using her dreams (being in the bedroom) would do it. By doing the six magic questions that we've done in the prison work section I would describe myself as one of many small frogs in a big pond or on a big wall. My purpose was to decorate the room. My biggest fear was to become faded, washed off the wall. My biggest hope was to get off on my own, be an independent frog like in those bedtime stories I'd heard in this room. Then I ask the dreamer to look at her life and see if any of these answers hit home. If I have trouble getting the dreamer to become the object, I let the whole group talk it through.

When you are presented with a short dream, it is interesting to use it in a dream theater. Have group members take the parts, allowing the dreamer to play herself. Do it again with the dreamer taking another part. Do it a third time, if necessary, with the dreamer taking yet another part. It is very powerful. This gets the group used to seeing the characters and objects from different points of view. It allows the dreamer easier access to the feelings of the other people and objects in the dream.

If you are working on your own, write a little story as each of these characters. See how the story changes when you write I am wallpaper with something missing. You might say something like I feel it is my job to cover everything yet part of me needs help sticking with the program. If it is your dream, this might be just the phrase that leads to an Aha. You may remember the one where the newspaper got in the dreamer's face shouting, "There's a sex offender in the area." It brought home to us how this dreamer was reliving problems she could do nothing about and acting this way had possibly led her mother's heart attack.

In a prison dream group, you get to offer a lot of advice. This has never been my strong suit but with a room full of people who've most likely experienced the same life experiences as the dreamer, advice comes from all of us, advice the girls take seriously. When complaints about guards come, I've used Mom-isms like 'don't bite the hand that feeds you'. I use gratitude lists to build a bridge away from negative thinking. I use the fact that if you hate someone, you are giving them power over your life, even if that person is unaware that you hate them. So, we talk about forgiveness, for ourselves so we can move on and change, and for others so they no longer have a hold on us. Asking forgiveness of their victims is a subject covered by other classes. We don't need to handle everything. All the women have had a chance to say whatever the words trigger in them. The dreamer knows the truth when she hears it. This way reinforces my hope that they feel they've found the message themselves; God has talked to them. They've also created a small community of like-minded friends in whom they can confide.

Lastly, have someone copy what you put on the board. During the next week you'll get a chance to think on these dreams and have even more insight. This gives you a good way to start the next session. You'll find the inmates also have further insight into their dreams.

Sometimes you get someone in class who doesn't believe they get dreams. The number one requirement to catching your dreams is to want to. It has to be a priority. Tell them to keep a pad and pen next to their bed, expecting a dream.

When you realize something is going through your head, about the time you think you need to go to the bathroom, stay where you are as long as you can, and keep replaying the scene in your head. Then when you get up to go to the bathroom, you'll be able to write the dream at the same time.

Next, listening to the group discuss dreams has led to a breakthrough in catching dreams for most of them. I've only had one who went the whole twelve weeks without recalling a dream. She developed an amazing ability to interpret dreams. Her ability to find metaphors and reasons why characters would possibly act the way they do was awesome. I believe she may be on her way to a new identity and career for herself. She surpassed my studied abilities and was very helpful back in her dorm.

CHAPTER THIRTY-TWO

The second night you'll probably delve deeper into nightmares and fear. I say probably because the concerns of the group will be your guide. Fear holds all of us back. The bible states 'fear not for God is with you'. In other words, if you have God you won't have fear. Looking at it another way, if you have fear, you don't have God! I would be the last to say I don't have God, yet, for some time in my life, fear ruled my dreams and my life, and I understand how hard it is to reach this new, safe place.

Many times I wake in the night, afraid, and asking, where's God? Of course He is with me. My fear was groundless. I learned to ask God to show me the dream message in a different way, one that did not frighten me. I'd either immediately see the message, or go back to sleep and get a different view of the same message.

I like to use the analogy of following someone down a path to get their attention. I call their name, no response. I shout their name, again no response. I see a large wooden log lying on the path, pick that up and hit the person over the head. This is my definition of a nightmare. How long has God been trying to get our attention? How long have we been ignoring Him?

When someone in dream group tells us they've had a nightmare I say "Oh goody!" Our biggest and quickest lessons to solve come in tension filled nightmares. When we get the message, the nightmare will not repeat and life will have improved – often with rewards. My experience with this process suggests everything wrong in life is due to wrong attitudes.

Prison personnel send women to me who scream all night, or put out a negative attitude all the time (maybe from lack of sleep) and I've had good luck with them. We talk of the effects of negative thinking, how they are contributing to their own personal illness; the benefit of keeping a gratitude journal. We try to find something to change their life patterns (like laughing). We do a lot of laughing in our dream group and find it enters into their dreams. It is so much more peaceful and healthier than fear.

As far as handling negative life patterns, the beauty of the group is that they can advise each other so much better than you or I, because they've experienced the same. They are quick to pick up on the symbols of the dreams, because they know each other so well. I continue to learn valuable lessons, each session we have.

Remember also the lady who received predictions and freaked out fearing they were the work of the devil. Truth is different for different people. Predictions are a way of life, the reason behind déjà vu. Some people believe we live everything in dreams before we do in life. This woman was responding to things the way her culture had taught her. No culture or religion holds all the answers. I find that we all tap into the energy field that holds energy from everything past, present and future that circles the earth. If I can find no personal reason for getting a prediction, I view the prediction as simply a marking of time.

Old cultures used dreams much more than we do. They assigned different deities to different actions, some were very frightening. My belief is that God is our creator and continues to work with us. I prefer to think of angels and loved ones passed over as having the time and caring about us enough to help us.

There are devils, many little ones to my estimation, but they only bother us when we invite them into our lives, such as putting harmful substances in our bodies, telling lies, willfully hurting others, gossiping, being negative, etc.

One tool to fight negativity is explaining the law of attraction. The movie 'The Secret' put out by a group called Spiritual Cinema, explains this best of any I've read or seen. Several people in this documentary show different ways we attract both good and bad into our lives. Even Oprah thought it important enough to devote three shows to it.

If you constantly think negative, you draw more negativity to yourself. If you constantly bemoan your aches and pains, you attract more aches and pains. The more laughter and love you build into your days, the more laughter and love you attract to yourself.

Studies have been done with water and its chemical makeup. Water changes according to the label put on its container, scientific fact. Since our bodies are a large percent of water, so do we change. As you think, so you are. Be careful how you label yourself.

I've witnessed wonderful changes in people simply by writing a gratitude list at the end of each day and reading it first thing in the morning. This is a good place to start with prison women. The chaplain had said there was nothing to be grateful for if you are in prison. The women in my group disagreed. They shouted out many things when we tried to do it as a group to show one inmate another way of thinking.

I suggest they keep a journal where they record their dreams. In the back I ask them to do three lists; 1) things they want to change about themselves, 2) things they want to bring into their lives, and 3) the gratitude list. It's amazing how fast we can cross things off the list when we start keeping track this way. It gives you a feeling that, yes, some unseen someone Is helping you.

If we have time, we like to meditate. I ask them to close their eyes, feet flat on the floor and take deep breaths. We relax the body beginning at the feet, squeeze and relax, the ankles, squeeze and relax, and on up the body. Then I take them mentally to someplace private for them like in a rain forest, a secluded pool, a rainbow. There I leave them with their thoughts and a connection with their subconscious. It is similar to dreaming but these are messages asked for, directed. While dreams can be directed, I believe it is of more benefit to let my subconscious tell me where I should be directing my energies; however, these mediation times can be very productive.

Remember the ocean and fish story told earlier in this book where, in meditation, the angry woman gave her anger to a big mouth bass and watched him swim away? It made a difference in her life.

Meditation is powerful. Often a dream will become clearer during the meditation. I like to call these meditation sessions power prayers. Healing of all kinds can take place.

As a handout this second class, I've suggested a set of dream work guidelines, both personal and group. A copy is in this handout section of this book.

CHAPTER THIRTY-THREE

Start each group meeting with a short lesson on dreams. An excellent idea by group meeting number three is to offer a handout with the names of inventors, writers, painters who've given credit to their dreams down through the ages. Einstein used to lay down on a couch when stuck on a problem and fall asleep with his arm out to the side, a small metal ball in his hand. When he fell asleep and the ball dropped onto the wooden floor, he'd wake up, contemplate the images that had been going through his mind, and find the answer. It is reported Edison did a similar exercise. He would fall asleep with his arm straight up in the air. When it fell, he'd go over what was going through his mind and he had his answer.

Elias Howe, while struggling over how to perfect the sewing machine, specifically how to get the thread to go through the material, fell asleep. He dreamed he was in a boiling cauldron with natives picking at him with spears. He noticed the spears had holes in the ends! He woke and wrote this down. The sewing machine needle was born.

Next on the agenda, ask if any of them have news regarding their dreams which you talked about the week before. Sometimes things have happened that clarify the dream. Sometimes the dreamer will have further ideas on the meaning of a symbol. It's a good time to share any further thoughts you might have had. We also use this time to share any news, job changes, family visits, and disciplinary actions (they've often been predicted in the dreams).

Then ask for the first dream. As it is told, write the key words on the board. Help them find a title for the dream. Not recommended is Trouble with Dad. It is too general and might be the title for several dreams. Use rather "dad eating a live frog." It's not likely to recur and could instantly bring the whole dream back to mind six months or a year from now.

Take a look at the theme of the dream. Perhaps the dream was about putting something where it doesn't belong. Maybe it is about frustration and they should look to some point in their life where they feel frustration. That could resonate with more than one of the group.

One other exciting thing about dreams is that we can learn from each other's dreams. Now you can lead them to start dissecting the symbols. I find that I often toss out an idea that takes off. The group's mind is tweaked and they come up with ideas of their own. Do as many dreams as you have or as time allows. If time is left over, meditate. Close with good wishes for all.

Session number four, lesson and handout, is about Jungian psychology. It helps them understand different meanings for different dream characters. I like to talk about Anima, Animus, shadow, joker, collective unconscious, archetypes, ego, persona, projection, complex, self, synchronicity.

Here, again, we delve into our inner selves and try to realize the why and wherefores of our behaviors. I shall include descriptions of these, a sample handout, at the end of this chapter.

This is one list that may demand more time, explain how the "I" figure can really be your higher self. Sometimes the frustration I've seen in my dreams was the frustration my guardian angel must have felt trying to lead me when I was not paying attention.

When dealing with all women, the animus occurs frequently in the guise of someone they know or once knew. Our lady throwing away the marijuana butts faced her animus (her opposite self) in the form of a man she detested. He was showing her who she need not become when she gave away her addition.

An archetype might show up as your mother, a baby, someone chasing you, finding food. These images are familiar to people all over this globe and from the beginning of time as evidenced by the drawings found on the walls of caves. Look at them not only to represent yourself but also your community, your nation, the world. The message could be universal, one that we all need to know.

The persona shows up in our clothing in the dream. It is what we think of ourselves. It's not always clothing, if you'll remember the shark story. Changing your clothes is significant of change coming in how you view yourself, how you present yourself to others. Being naked is about not hiding anything, being your true self. That's good. Often in the dream you'll feel embarrassment at being naked. It's only because you've been living a lie for so long. You've been wearing clothes that represented images of who you thought you should be, ideas that were impressed upon you through your upbringing.

Projection is one of my favorites. Each character or thing, even a suitcase is you. You must project yourself into the feelings of each of these in a dream. If a suitcase is in the dream, is it being stuffed into a closet? Is it being kicked around or ignored? When in your life do you feel the same/

I have a favorite story about projection. My dog is a breed that has inbred training to attack other dogs to protect sheep. She is more people than dog. It came to me that this is a perfect example of projection. She does not want to think of herself as a dog. So when she sees a dog she gets angry. She hates them. One woman told of a hate (and that is not a strong enough word) she felt for a new person in her dorm. She knew this was an unreasonable reaction. The thing is projection. She sensed in this person something she won't admit to in herself. She needs to face facts and deal with whatever this is. She held onto the hate, instead, until she was transferred to another dorm.

Self is the word Jung gave to that mysterious someone who brings us all we need to know, in our dreams. My word is God. Some refer to this as our higher self. When doing dream work you often need someone to thank, and this is it. Thank him\her\it each time you have remembered a dream long enough to write it down. Thank her for the message. Ask her for further insights.

Shadow is the name Jung gives to those parts of ourselves we don't want to recognize. It is not always bad. My best shadows were things I didn't know about myself that led to better things when I took a look at them and made them a part of my life. Sometimes it is things you want to hide. Nothing is forbidden between you and your creator. God won't bring you anything you can't handle. Don't be afraid to consider why this image is being brought back to your memory.

Lastly is synchronicity. Before we talked of the lady who, because of the teaching of her culture, freaked out when she got predictions. It is a way of life and most of us marvel in this part of life. It shows a power greater than us at work. It reminds us all is as planned with the world. God is in charge, we are helping. It just needs more of us tuned in to our inner selves, tuned in to our creator, tuned in to helping him\her improve conditions everywhere. We can co-create our day.

CHAPTER THIRTY-FOUR

During my fifth class I usually hand out a color chart developed by Robert J. Hoss, author of <u>Dream Language; Self-Understanding Through Imagery and Color</u>. You can find the chart and copy it from that book. He has a website and you can also find it in most book stores and on Amazon.com. Another place is on the IASD (International Association For the Study Of Dreams) website.

Although it may be called for earlier in the session, like any other dream dictionary, it is better to learn to stretch our minds and be able to think beyond any guide. Stretch minds by practicing coming up with meanings on your own for different colors and symbols.

My approach has sprung from my early training in meditation where if I surrounded myself in green it was healing and growth. If I surrounded myself in blue it was peace, a peace I needed or the world needed. It was an invitation to my Creator to let wisdom deep within me come to the service of my mind. If I was in a place of red or wearing red, it was passion, pink was love, yellow was job, white was purity and holiness, brown was of the earth, black was the unconscious. This has served me well although reading Bob's sentences about each color has helped others.

Practice coming up with your\their own interpretations before turning to dictionaries. You can get stuck, with dictionaries, relying on their words and not exercising your own resources. They seldom have all the answers. Later they may be used as a step to stimulate your mind.

Also on this night I hand out the six magic questions. We've already worked with them but Robert J. Hoss developed them and they are on the back of his color handout.

The universe will bring you stories, poems, and art to share. The group members bring things that I've taken home, copied and given to each of them.

Another topic you might research is the difference between male and female energy. Male, or the man in your dream, is pointing out something you either lack, or have too much of. He is encouraging you to go in a specific direction – or stay away from the direction.

I'm thinking of the marijuana butts and the man the dreamer absolutely would not admit was a part of her. In the dream, this character was reminding her not to go in that direction or she may end up like him. Male is the thinking side where female is the feeling side. We all have some of each. Our dreamer, in this instance, was feeling the revulsion she felt for this person when in truth, he really was an archetype, or a messenger from God, in disguise, coming or sent to help her over some hurdle. By remembering this dream, she has added a strength of character to her waking persona that was much needed.

An old myth, about the time when the world was populated by gods, has them creating a human being with two heads, four arms and four legs. You can still see this symbol today in medical journals. It was both male and female. It was the perfect being and the gods were jealous of its peace, contentment, and happiness. They decided to cut it in half. However, it had been given a soul and that could not be cut in half. Now we spend our lives looking for our soul mate. We look to every other human creature when the truth is that we can find that complete being only inside ourselves. The mystery of who we really are is within, visible in our dreams and contemplations. When you come to know yourself, to love yourself, then, you will be able to fully love others.

The sixth session brings together all we've tried to learn. I bring in a short movie, I joined The Spiritual Cinema Circle. It's like a book of the month club but they send you inspirational movies; shorts, documentaries and features. If you are interested in learning more about them go to www.SpiritualCinemaCircle.com.

Once or twice each session we clear a night to view a short movie and discuss it as if it were a dream. One of the first I used was a short 15 minute film entitled Amal. It is about an East Indian man who drives a taxi for a living and appears to be very happy. He is honest to a fault which earns him a place in a rich customer's will. He has a friend, a fellow taxi driver who is constantly taking advantage of his good nature, sometimes even stealing from him. When the old man dies, a female lawyer hunts Amal down and gives him proof of his inheritance on a paper which he throws away to a little girl, a street urchin, who wants to return it to him but his friend enlightens us to the fact that Amal can't read.

The ending of this film brought a huge gasp of empathetic feeling to the prison women. Then we began dissecting the film as if it were our dream.

The film already had a title, an important part of a dream. Can this group come up with a more appropriate name? "Wish I was a Little Girl?" She ended up with the riches – assuming it were possible to spread the riches by giving that piece of paper away. Next let's look for a theme. Hard work may make you miss the mark? Take time to really see the world around you? Can I work a little learning into my life? Never stop learning! Open other doors of your mind!

I see the friend as the shadow character of the dream. He is interesting because we all have a part buried inside us (sometimes not buried far enough) that tries to cause ourselves harm. You've heard the phrase that we can be our own worst enemy? If it were my dream and I was the other taxi driver, I'd look to what I may be doing in life that is hurting myself rather than helping myself. This struck home with the prison women.

If it were my dream and I was the will, I'd look to someplace in my life where I feel I have potential but no one is noticing me or giving me a chance. I have a lot to offer and do not need to be bounced from pillar to post.

I see the rich old man as God, the giver of all things wonderful. He is also a part of me. The answer is inside me. He rides in my car of life. The riches of the will are inside me.

There are two female parts in this movie, the lawyer tracking down Amal and the little girl street urchin. If it were my dream and I was Amal, the lawyer would be my Anima or opposite. She represents what an education would do for me and, perhaps, is trying to push Amal in the direction.

Looking for more Jungian characters we find the hard work and dedication Amal puts forth as complexes. Somewhere deep in his subconscious is this complex (we have more than one) that he must be a cab driver and work night and day competing for fares by being honest and always there. Perhaps he is following a family tradition. This is good but it is not all there is to life.

The little girl represents Amal's female side which is small, not developed. He believes this is all there is to life for him. It's not working the dream because he has no time to go home, to be with his family. He moves like a horse with blinders. Yet this small bit of female is there inside him, trying to get his attention.

While it is fascinating to have the glimpse of life in modern India, the many messages when this is worked as a dream help us with our own lives and the exercise helps us dissect our own dreams better. It pays to occasionally step back from metaphor and gut feeling and take a real clinical look at one of our dreams. This keeps us from getting into a rut and possibly overlooking the real message.

We, in the prison group, have a lot of fish in our dreams. Another film from Spiritual Cinema that I like to go over with them is entitled Einstein. Einstein is a fish that needs someone to look after him while his owner goes on vacation. The chore is thrust on a reclusive female neighbor. The neighbor ends up loving this gold fish, taking it, in its bowl of water, everywhere.

It is a story of personal growth and I'm hoping it will shed some light on our own fish symbols.

CHAPTER THIRTY-FIVE

If you don't have access to movies or a TV\DVD player to show them, try taking a look at short stories. Bring in a story that you pass around allowing more than one person to read. Meanwhile, as in analysis, write the key words on the board. And work at interpreting the dream or story from each characters view point.

Another fun way to achieve this same goal is to follow the story of the Wizard of Oz. For the few who never heard it, the group will soon bring them up to speed. We've done this with a lot of laughter and enthusiasm. If you were the dog Toto, perhaps you are hanging out with the wrong crowd on this fools mission. Maybe, somewhere in your life, you are too trusting and loyal.

If you are the munchkins, you are being shown a large part of yourself that is cheering you on, wanting the best for you. The Tin Man, Scare Crow and Lion are also parts of yourself from whom you can learn. The yellow brick road and the Emerald City have shown up in our own dreams in many ways. It is like they are modern archetypes.

I like Dorothy because, to me, she admits she's lost. Am I lost in life? I don't know everything and am willing to ask direction. If you'll remember, once again, the inmate picking the butts out of the ashtray, you'll remember it was emerald green in color. We believed the dream was also saying to clean up this bowl of her life, find her own Emerald City!

When another inmate had a vision of one lock of blonde hair curling tight in a circle, we found the yellow brick road in this image and hoped it meant she was on the right path.

A discussion of modern archetypes can be interesting. At least keep track of any unusual images you find. In a discussion with other dream group leaders, this could be very helpful. The transformers children play with are appearing in children's dreams. Children go through a lot more transformation than adults and a lot faster.

In our prison dreams, I've noticed a few DVDs or CDs being burned, recording new memories over old, perhaps. Think before following through on a dream image. Do you want this in your memory banks forever? You'll let the concerns of your group help you decide which subject to teach them.

Another tool that can't be stressed enough is our ability to ask questions of our dreams and get answers. I used this often the first two years of my own dream work. We can go into meditation with a question on our minds or we can go to sleep with the question. Some samples of questions might be; why did I react the way I did? Why can't I get along with my sister? Is she right? Do I need to change my diet? What should I do next? How do I get through these next days? Am I on the right path? What sort of picture would look best over the sofa?

No concern of yours is too great or too small for the master of your dreams to express an opinion.

Take one question at a time, write it on a piece of paper. Wording is important. I've repeated a question a second night, with a slight word change, hoping to get a better answer, and it worked. It's like asking may I or can I. Of course you can. Should you may be another matter.

Hold the paper in your hands and pray asking God the same question. Your depth of feeling has a lot to do with whether you get an answer or not. I've found that what is important to me is not what God feels is most important in my life and gotten a dream story that I could only translate toward and unthought-of-direction.

The dream you get may be a straight out answer or it may be a story you need to translate. Remember, God works with your emotions, feelings. If, for instance, I'd had an argument and wanted to know who was right and who was wrong, I often got a third answer. It usually was a dream showing a third point of view, or another story entirely, showing me how petty this was to argue about in the whole picture of what was important to my life at that time. I may get a story that showed where the other person was coming from, why she felt this way, what in her childhood made her react this way. I'd come away feeling empathy for this person.

You might follow with the question; what do you want me to do next?

If you wake from a high energy dream and are puzzled, ask God to give you the same message another way. I can remember having a dream that bothered me, perhaps a nightmare, and ended up sitting on the floor next to my bed. In the middle of the night, I'm sitting there, leaning up against the bed while my husband slept peacefully on the other side of the bed. I asked God to tell me the message in a way that didn't frighten me, a way I might easily understand. When I climbed back in bed and fell asleep, He gave me another message that was entirely different yet related.

Especially with prisoners, when they become depressed over loved ones, their children or parents; have them ask God for information about them. They will have them in their dreams and feel much better for it.

You can ask your dreams questions like why the disaster of September 11, 2001 (for instance) or why the tsunami that wiped out so many people happened. When I asked about that I dreamed that I was overlooking a garden with another person. I believe that to have been God. We watched a tall set of concrete steps leading up to a mansion. At the top of the steps were four Hollywood people. They put on a show and danced down the ledge that bordered the steps. God said to me, "Now everyone will think that is the way to climb those steps." In other words, we're following the wrong set of ideals.

Often the dreams will seem not to have answered your request. Write it anyway. On deciphering it later, you will be amazed at the truth of the messages that come through.

We humans are putting the wrong images as our priority, God made a solid set of steps for us to climb. Because of free will we often follow the wrong teachers, set the wrong priorities, and walk the wrong path. We try to skirt the issues by sliding along the edges and not walking directly on the steps.

On a lighter side, this seems to be getting very serious for me and, there is a light side. While visiting my daughter's new home for the first time, I walked into the front door which is half way between the upper and lower levels, a raised ranch. There is a tall, empty wall above my head where she expressed a desire to paint something of her own to put there. She had a woodsy image in mind that had meaning from her childhood.

That night, the perfect image came to me in a dream (at least I thought so). It was to do the sketch and pick out three parts of it to transfer onto unframed canvases that would stagger its' way up this tall wall, like meandering through the woods. Time will tell how she will handle it but this is a good example of the master of our dreams trying to solve the small problems of our days. This is the source of writers, inventors and people of vision the world over.

When I have doubts as to my ability to handle a touchy situation, I sleep on it. The answer magically appears the next morning. Never forget to thank that unseen helper. My mantra is "Thank you God, thank you God, thank you God!"

Some dream workers will talk about confidentiality. Confidentiality is good but how is this work to be spread if we don't talk about it. Isn't the greater good of educating as many people as possible to the fact that they can have two-way communication with our creator more important? When talking about other peoples' dreams, I never tell their name. If there is a place mentioned, I change the place. This sacred communication is meant to be shared. It is often a lesson in living that applies to more than one person.

Last but not least, if a dream is bothersome, high energy and has no end, go back to sleep and dream an ending. Write an ending you'd like to have. It helps.

CHAPTER THIRTY-SIX

Death is another place where cultures collide and personal experience must be allowed to speak to us. Death comes in dreams quite often, our own death, someone else's death, or someone who has died. How do we handle it? A friend of mine reported a most wonderful dream just this morning. She became aware she was dreaming by vibrations, tingling, around the top of her head. Next she became aware of walking into a boardroom. The man in charge asked her if she wanted to go now or stay a while longer. She replied that she wanted to stay.

This brings up many questions about what we've been led to believe. Was she visiting heaven and the deity (or gatekeeper) in charge of coming and going? Are we given a choice of when we want to leave this earth? If we can visit loved ones who've died, do they sometimes visit us? So many people have reported dreams where a loved one who has died has been showing he is well and happy. If the dreamer finds comfort in this, it is good.

People long for messages from loved ones on the other side. When it comes they feel great joy and relief. Is this bad? Not at all. You might be asking, what about judgment day? Some theologies say we all wait for everyone else for a joint judgment day. My belief has evolved past these teachings from my childhood to believe every day on earth is judgment day. We have the opportunity, up until our so called death, to make our choices here on earth, judge ourselves while here. This goes along with the theory that life on earth is a learning experience. Looks like St. Peter just lost a job. I'm sure heaven is full of more levels of bureaucracy than we ever thought of. There is a job for all, but it will be something we love to do.

EPILOGUE

The Rest of the Story

My prison ministry (in this form) is no more. There are too many people, with more influence than I, who do not want to realize the benefits, the opportunities for rehabilitation that working with dreams in a group setting can bring. Church volunteers may center on declining social values but these stories you've read in this book point to a deeper problem. That is the absence of any feeling of self-worth in these people. My work outside the prison often points to the same problem there. We don't grow up knowing who we really are!

One of the ladies relieved of nightly demons declined further help with her dreams. She said she was nothing but a pervert. She was much too young and innocent about life to accept that label. I wished I'd had more time with her.

Religion and bible study are good but what happens when the inmate is back out on the streets? Who helps her juggle finding a place to live, buying clothes, eating, taking care of her children's needs? I can understand how they fall back into what they know.

Where are these loving people, who volunteer so much time in the prison and teach so lovingly about God and church, then?

Dream study leads to a shift in perception of who they are and this can lead them in different directions when they get out, as you've read. We've seen rewards miraculously appear when they tuned into their inner selves. They no longer need to feel alone in this world.

The girls began telling me that as soon as they signed the list for my class they were approached by other inmates and volunteers and told not to take my class. I could often tell whenever a new person had received this treatment because they showed up with a thick Bible in hand. They were told the devil was in this room.

Unfortunately, I lost the battle. My dream is now to get five copies of this book in each prison library so those interested can learn from them. When I accomplish this – who is the winner then? All of us.

One of the unbelievers in the value of dreams walked into the prison with me one night. She was there to mentor an inmate. She asked what I did and when I told her she whipped out a leaflet against dreams so fast, she had to have been anticipating meeting me. I saw a circle with words radiating out from it with words like dreams and devil. I refused to take it. I told her that was judging and the Bible had clear words against judging others. She allowed me to walk away without a further word.

Another time, in class, one of the inmates came running back from what was supposed to be a trip to the bathroom that was in the chapel building. She was shocked, all color gone from her face at what she'd witnessed going on in the chapel. She said that inmates were screaming and rolling around on the floor as volunteers appeared to be beating the devil out of them, blowing horns and beating drums over them. I learned later these volunteers, from this church group, 'knew' nightmares were of the devil and they were probably trying to beat the literal devil out of the girls. My teaching that nightmares are a tool of God, a tool to wake us up to some important life change that needs to be made, goes against all their teaching.

I eventually made a handout of my own, printed on tough photographic paper and handed them out to my class, ten to an inmate. They disappeared fast and the girls asked for more the next week. They not only gave them out in prison but sent them home.

My handout told them that they had asked me to read Dt. 13: vs 1-5 about all prophets and dreamers being put to death. I asked them to read Dt. 1 to see where in time this is taking place and see that Moses is the speaker of these words. I asked them to read a little further and see the troubles that Moses feared would befall his community when he died and someone else was leading them.

Nowhere in the Bible does it say not to be your own prophet, study your own dreams. Several places it encourages you to do so. I've read that there are over seven hundred dreams and miracles in the Bible. I ask them to look in a couple of places where God says those who did not listen to the prophets would be punished. We are born with this ability. Use it. Read 1Cor. 14:vs. 26-39, read Rev. 18:vs 20, read Acts 2:vs 17, read Matthew 5 vs. 11 & 12, 17, Luke 11 vs 49-52.

A little more about the women I've taught. One girl I've known from the beginning has moved to another prison. We exchange letters about twice a month and she should be out in another two years. Two women have died, both seemingly of liver cancer. I say seemingly because my information comes via the inmate's grapevine.

One of the dead was also with me from the beginning of my classes. I came to appreciate her greatly. I've tried without success to locate her family, let them hear some good things about her. She is the one whose grandmother sent in dreams for the group to interpret. It seems her last dream talked about in class was prophetic. It included a fish lying on a lunch counter, out of water and soon to be eaten.

The other made a wonderful connection with God. She saw hands reaching down from above helping her make a connection. She was the grateful recipient, after that dream, of a couple of rewards. She was finally allowed to communicate with her son who was also in prison, and she was invited to take part in the culinary arts program.

These rewards have happened time after time, just for finally learning to access your inner, higher voice. It's happened to me. Next is a gift for you – some handouts to copy and use in your own dream work.

HANDOUTS

Please feel free to copy.

Bible Dreams and Visions

I've heard it said that if we take the dreams and visions out of the Bible, we wouldn't have much of a book. Dreams, as we all know, did not stop with the death of Christ. In fact, he is quoted as saying others would come after him. I believe they have been coming, for a long time, in our dreams and intuitions.

These listing are but a few.

Old Testament

Abraham's dream vision	Genesis 15:12-21
Jacob's dream	Genesis 28:10-22
Joseph's use of dreams	Genesis 37:5-11
	Genesis 40 & 41
Solomon's Dream 1	Kings 3:5-15
Samuel's call 1	Samuel 3::3-14
Eliphaz's dream	Job 4:12-21
Isaiah's call	Isaiah 6:1-13
Ezekiel's call	Ezekiel 1::4-3:3
Daniel and dreams	Daniel 2-4

New Testament

Joseph's dream of Mary	Matthew 1:20-21
Joseph's other dreams	Matthew 2:1-13, 19-20
Baptism of Jesus	Matthew 3:16-17
Zechariah's vision	Luke 1:11-20

Shepherd's vision	Luke 2:8-14
Transfiguration	Luke 9:28-36
Paul's conversion vision	Acts 9:3-9
Peter's dream vision	Acts 10:3-21
Paul's night visions	Acts 16:9,18:9,23:1,27:23

Many of Jesus' parables lend themselves well to dream work. Our own dreams can be considered parables, especially when they have a universal theme that can fit anyone.

DREAM GROUPS

BELIEFS
1) You'll find a wise person in your dreams who knows all about you and loves you no matter what. This wise person wants to make your life better.
2) That wise person has been called many things. You may call it what you want, spirit, she,. I say God. The important thing is to know it.
3) We are alive to learn to work with this Spirit.
4) The best for you is the best for spirit. Your best means health, success, happiness that comes from fulfilling your purpose of being.

NIGHTMARES
1) This loving being will not give you more than you can handle. Trust in this. You have the power to tell demons to go away.
2) Demons come to teach lessons and you learn.
3) Nightmares can be God's tools. Write them down and find meaning. Defeat them and get on to those better things life has to offer.
4) Don't be afraid to tell God how you feel. He knows, but may not trust you to follow through.

DREAMS
1) "Dreams use what you know to tell you what you don't know." Jeremy Taylor; and "All dreams come in service for health and wholeness."
2) The true messages come through as images.
3) Images evoke emotions. Changes come not through thinking things out but through your heart.

4) Every person and thing in the dream is you. "Close your eyes and become one of the images. Describe yourself.

WHAT ARE YOU TRYING TO FEEL, DO, SAY?
What do you like best about being this thing? What do you dislike about being this thing? What is your biggest fear? What is your fondest wish?

Dream Group Work; can be used in private also.

1) There are no absolute interpretations. Each of our beginnings and experiences, while similar, are different, and they can change. The dreamer will receive an "Aha" when the truth is made known.
2) We don't tell someone how to live their life. We don't judge.
3) We look toward associations, plays on words, if approaching this alone, it's helpful to have at least one other trusted person to pass the dream by and get their opinion.
4) So we do not judge someone else's circumstances, we say "If it were my dream, it might mean . . . ."

*Robert J. Hoss, Dream Language: Self Understanding through Imagery and Color

FAMOUS PEOPLE WHO USED DREAMS

If nothing else, many writers over the years have credited their dreams with inspiration for books. Most notable among present day writers is Stephen King. He found a way to enlist the aid of his mentor of the night to make him prolific and rich. This gift of dreaming was given to you at birth. It costs nothing. Why not use it?

A newer writer who credits his dreams is Neal Donald Walsh with his Conversation From God. Another writer was Samuel Clemens, a.k.a. Mark Twain, Edgar Allen Poe, Mary Shelley wrote Frankenstein, and Robert Louis Stevenson. Charlotte Bronte used dreams to write Jane Eyre. Also, a Nobel Peace Prize winner, Henri Bergson wrote that common sense was more available in the sleep state. When you search, you'll find many. Artists are also inspired by dreams, Salvador Dali for one. Ask most American Indians where their inspiration for art comes and you'll hear a story of a dream.

Film makers and directors who credit their dreams include Orson Welles, Carlos Saura, Ingmar Bergman. Musicians include Richard Wagner who wrote Tristan Da Isolde, George Frederic Handel known for his Messiah, and more. A man named Sullivan is known for composing The Last Chord from a dream. Better known to us, perhaps is comedian\composer Steve Allen.

Athletes, like golfer Jack Nicklaus, talked about using their dreams to overcome a slump, improve their game. Other great people who used dreams for guidance include Harriet Tubman. She led hundreds of other slaves to freedom by means of what we today call the Underground Railway. Her dreams always helped her find safe passageways and she never lost a single person. Mahatma Gandhi is known for his nonviolent freeing of India from English rule. Martin Luther King followed his example and used the words, "I have a dream." A dream experienced by President Lyndon Johnson contributed to the withdrawal of our troops from Viet Nam. He dreamed he was trying to swim across a river but got caught up in a circular movement. Round and round he swam. On waking, he knew he had to get out of the situation this country was in to reach the side of peace. He spoke often to his staff of his dreams.

We all recall that Abraham Lincoln was warned of his death in a dream. Surprisingly, big tough guy, General George S. Patton frequently called his personal secretary, Joe Rosevich, in the middle of the night to dictate battle plans.

Inventors, scientists, mathematicians used dreams. Elias Howe, stuck while trying to make his invention of a sewing machine work, went to sleep to dream of a band of cannibals cooking him in a huge pot. As they jabbed their spears at him, he noticed holes in the ends of the spears. He woke, knowing he had his answer.

Einstein is said to purposely fall asleep when he was stuck in a premise. He'd lie on a bed, his arm outstretched with a metal ball in his hand. When the ball fell, Einstein woke and wrote what was going through his mind. He had his answer. Thomas Edison held his arm up in the air. As he fell asleep the arm would fall and Edison would write whatever was going through his mind. A NASA scientist was recently written up in a scientific journal about his use of dreams.

A wealth of material on this can be found in "Our Dreaming Mind", a book by Robert L. Van De Castle, PH.D. The unseen ether that circles the earth holding all knowledge is open to each of us smart enough to tap in. Give it a try!

GLOSSARY OF JUNGIAN TERMS

The first two show up in the dreams of men or women, as their counterpart. It could be someone you know, a wise old person, a child, an authority figure, a movie star. Watch where this person is trying to lead you, the example he\she may be trying to set for you. Try to see things from his\her perspective and incorporate that attitude into your life.

Anima: (Latin, "Soul") Is the subconscious, feminine side of a man's personality. She is personified in dreams by images of females ranging from child to seductress to spiritual guide. A man's anima development is reflected in how he relates to women.

Animus: (Latin, "Spirit") Is the subconscious, masculine side of a woman's personality. The animus is personified in women's dreams by images ranging from muscle-men to poets to spiritual leaders. A woman's animus development is reflected in how she relates to men.

Archetypes: These appear as images and ideas, universal patterns or motifs present in the collective subconscious. Archetypal images are the basic content of religion, mythology and art. An archetype brings in whatever complex you need to see with different eyes.

Complex: Is an emotionally charged group of ideas or images. At the core of a complex is an archetypal image. (See shadow.)

Ego: You, but not you. The worker, the planner, the diaper changer, the sum of who you think you are. Often the "I" of a dream. We can change our ego, give it less or more power, if and when the ego agrees, but – is this the truth? Look to "Self" below.

Persona: (Latin "actor's mask) One's social role, derived from the expectations of society and early training. It is useful both in facilitating contact with others and as a protective covering. Identification with a particular persona can slow or stop psychological development. In dreams, clothes are a clue to persona. Ever wonder what people see when they look at you?

Projection: A natural process whereby a subconscious characteristic of one's own is perceived in an outer object or person. If you are highly bothered by someone else's action, it most likely is because that trait is within yourself, and you don't want to see it.

Self: The archetype of wholeness and the regulating center of the psyche, experienced as a numinous power that transcends the ego (e.g., God).

Shadow: A mainly subconscious part of the personality, characterized by traits and attitudes, both negative and positive, which the ego tends to reject or ignore. This is really the starting place for self-study. Your shadow holds the complexes, engages the archetype to bring you the message to kill or cure or incorporate. Once known, they can bring great good into your life.

Synchronicity: A meaningful coincidence between an event in the outside world and a dream or meditation or active imagination state.

SOURCES

People quoted, ideas learned from;

*Page 81 – November 30, 200g Justice Department report, Tampa Tribute copied from the December 1, 2006 Washington Post article that 1 in 32 people in the United States are either in jail, on probation, or on parole.]

*All scripture is taken from the NIV Study Bible; 10th Anniversary Edition, International Version, Zondervan

*Haden Institute Greenville, North Carolina
Degrees in Dream Leader Training and Spiritual Direction
www.hadeninstitute.com

*Robert Van de Castle, PhD,.
www.ourdreamingmind.com

*Robert J. Joss, MS, Author
www.dreamscience.org

*Jeremy Taylor, Rev. Author
www.jeremytaylor.com

*International Association for The Study of dreams (IASD)

www.asdreams.org
*Spiritual Cinema
Films that inspire love and compassion
www.spiritualcinemacircle.com

ABOUT THE AUTHOR

Carol Oschmann began dream study to rid herself of stress. Her nightmares were the one thing she might be able to control. After reading "Edgar Cayce on Dreams," she adopted the belief that God talks to you in dreams. It confirmed a message she'd heard from a minister when she visited a Baptist Church. He said, "I don't know how God talks to you, but He talks to me in my dreams." Her rewards have been many.

Born in upstate New York, the mother of three and grandmother of four, great grand-mother of five, a bookkeeper by trade, she was amazed as her life shifted to that of a writer and photographer for a travel magazine, program planner for a T.V. travel program, and dream researcher.

Most amazing of all, to her, was her new ability to dream for other people.

For a complete guide to her spiritual development read her latest book, "When God Stood Up." Carol is a graduate of the Haden Institute and is a Dream Group Leader. She leads a weekly dream study group in Sun City Center, Florida, has led one in Brandon, Florida, and one at a correctional facility in Florida. She also teaches a six-week course on the subject. Carol writes occasionally for Dream Network Magazine and promotes her lecture business. She has given talks on dreams before church groups, senior groups, college alumni groups, Lions Clubs, rotaries, community women's groups, and others. She's talked in churches, college dorms, homes, restaurants and apartment recreation rooms.

Carol's services as a dreamer can be found on her website, www.caroloschmann.com.

www.ingramcontent.com/pod-product-compliance
Lightning Source LLC
LaVergne TN
LVHW040141080526
838202LV00042B/2982